# WOMEN IN LOVE WITH THE DIVINE

# WOMEN IN LOVE WITH THE DIVINE

## A Seeker's Exploration of Faith, Practice, and Feminine Power

ERICA BASSANI

SHAMBHALA

Shambhala Publications, Inc.
2129 13th Street
Boulder, Colorado 80302
www.shambhala.com



Cover art: iStock.com/NSA Digital Archive
Cover design: Lauren Michelle Smith
Interior design: Lauren Michelle Smith



9 8 7 6 5 4 3 2 1

First Edition
Printed in the United States of America

Shambhala Publications makes every effort to print on acid-free, recycled paper.

Shambhala Publications is distributed worldwide by Penguin Random House, Inc., and its subsidiaries.

LIBRARY OF CONGRESS CATALOGING-IN-PUBLICATION DATA
Names: Bassani, Erica author
Title: Women in love with the divine: a seeker's exploration of faith, practice, and feminine power / Erica Bassani.
Description: First edition. | Boulder, Colorado: Shambhala, [2026] |
Identifiers: LCCN 2025023478 | ISBN 9781645474425 trade paperback
Subjects: LCSH: Christian women—Religious life | Women teachers—Religious life | Love—Religious aspects—Christianity
Classification: LCC BV4527 .B3748 2026 |
DDC 248.8/43—dc23/eng/20250812
LC record available at https://lccn.loc.gov/2025023478

The authorized representative in the EU for product safety and compliance is eucomply OÜ, Pärnu mnt 139b-14, 11317 Tallinn, Estonia, hello@eucompliancepartner.com.

*It was life that gave me this project to which I would otherwise never have dared to devote myself. I am here to honor, encourage, and promote the inner quest of soft strength, deep balance among polarities, and all-embracing knowledge. Guiding us will be the voices of women who dedicate their lives to the Divine. The journey begins with the call. The times are calling us. Nature is calling us. The drum of the sleeping heart, the mountains that are the sovereigns of this earth, and the imbalanced dance of all phenomena are calling us to awaken to the soul of the world.*

*May we all realize our true nature.*

# CONTENTS

PART THREE

## BIRTH 123

# INITIATION

When I started writing this book, it seemed like a simple enough endeavor. I had no idea of the challenges I would have to face to accomplish it. Now that the book is complete, the experience of birthing it feels more like a survival challenge that I evidently passed—thanks to faith and the help of the countless kind and compassionate beings who supported me. (The world is so full of people with hearts of gold.)

This book was born in India, in Rishikesh to be exact, at a time when all seemed lost. In truth, it was more like I relinquished my familiar world rather than lost it. Yet because I hadn't directly acknowledged that to myself, it seemed like a life-orchestrated conspiracy, a betrayal. I had left my cherished attic nest in Turin and my beloved partner, brutally and remotely, within the span of a month—without really knowing why. All I knew is that I had a feeling that it was "the right thing to do." Of course, I had been the one moving objects around the attic, filling cardboard boxes with aged books, bohemian clothes, and scented candles. I was the one who put an end to a love story that too often felt like a trap, a psychological marathon. But the truth is that I was feeling pushed by invisible hands toward making a leap into the void that I had absolutely no desire to take.

Other parts of my life also conspired to change. Each day I dedicated a few hours to a monotonous online writing job that AI could have easily handled. Eventually, it did indeed replace me. My spiritual practice was also adrift: after eight years of intense Buddhist practice and daily meditation; after almost becoming a nun in the Thai Forest tradition of Theravada Buddhism; after several vipassana, loving-kindness, and winter retreats; after absorbing endless Dharma talks on impermanence, nonself, and cessation, I sat in meditation with ambiguous chaos. Every attempt I made to be with this chaos was washed away by unrecognizable waves that rolled over me, leaving me overwhelmed by the debris they left behind.

In an attempt to regain my center, I immersed myself in an intensive yoga retreat in Rishikesh. I hoped that strengthening my limbs would help me stay afloat. But this roiling sea left me lying for weeks on a ruthless Indian bed with a vertebra out of place. I had no choice but to draw the curtains and reflect on my life—the agony of this was interrupted only by visits from my beloved retreat sisters, who would come to deliver peanut butter, papaya, and compassion.

The "me" I had constructed began to crumble. I felt it drifting away, pulled by a formless, boundless, inexorable tide. Every emotion, every thought, every memory was taken by a flood as if it were an umbrella, a table, or a piano—objects that had once inhabited a house of which I had been the undisputed mistress. It was a process over which I had no control—a formidable and profound convulsion.

I call that period, for which nothing and no one had prepared me, the Great Flood. A dam of cosmic proportions—one that had always existed within me but of which I knew nothing—had broken. Where did this dam come from? Had I created it over the years, like a mad architect working at night on a plan to contain the uncontainable? It was disarming to discover all the years of practice I had done could not help me at that moment. Self-discipline, structure, and rigorous practice were no longer helpful. I could only surrender to the feeling of having no way out and sink into helplessness. I waited, powerless, for a miracle to happen.

The first miracle was that my back returned to normal thanks to the intervention of a yoga teacher in the tradition of Iyengar, which is known for its capacity to bring one back into alignment. Nonetheless, here I was in the Indian capital of yoga, amid proud performers and supple seekers, with my body strained, exhausted, depleted. I found myself in the grip of a nagging thought: *What is the point of moving?* This became a looming existential question. I found myself, like a deflated balloon, resting on the shore of the Ganges River, considered to be the manifestation of the Divine Mother. In her empathetic presence, I sat there at sunset, full of ancient pain, with tears that came from who knows where and from who knows when. When it felt like this mysterious pain would sweep me away, I stepped into the cold running water and asked the sacred Ganges to hold me steady. Despite the current, my feet never slipped off the stones. With my head below the surface, I asked Ganga Mata (Mother Ganga) to keep the pieces of myself and turn me into water. (I assure you; I had never talked to a river before.) But wherever I went, the pain followed me. No matter what I did, the tears flowed, warm and powerful, relentlessly bringing to the surface buried stories and memories. So, I kept coming back to the Ganges as if nothing else were real.

I admired the Indian devotees who filled copper bowls at the river and talked to God through the water. They knew exactly how many magical syllables must be said and how many times the prayers must be repeated. It seemed to me that everyone had been instructed on how to remedy the inconveniences of chance and be supported by the sky. My recipe for well-being, on the other hand, had been borne away in the Great Flood. It was in that state of utter helplessness that I perceived, for the first time, the Divine Mother as a living, breathing, yet ungraspable entity. I began to glimpse the Divine as the eternal essence that flows everywhere and fills everything with endless love, constantly giving birth to perception. I asked Her to show me the substance that sustains us, to reveal what lies behind everything, to help me understand what this mysterious thing is that everything appears in. I begged Her to show me how to find refuge when a storm washes us adrift, without anything to hold on to.

An autonomous will, at first gentle and then increasingly energetic and powerful, began to make its way—daring and pushing—through the rubble inside me. Life, a powerful force beyond my control, began to flow again and gave me a great reason to move on into the sacred unknown. This was the second miracle I witnessed: My vital forces had returned, accompanied by a new sense of purpose—a mission I had not chosen.

With the love of Ganga Mata holding me afloat, I had a strong desire to meet women who had found ultimate refuge in the Divine and discuss with them questions like: How do women uniquely experience and connect with the Divine? How can women honor their spiritual path while navigating cultural constraints and personal challenges? How might we heal ancient feminine wounds without falling into the trap of vindication and resentment? How can the tradition of feminine wisdom help us investigate the Divine mystery in today's world? How can we grow freely and without shame into a greater blossoming awareness of who we are?

Rishikesh swirled around me. Each evening at five o'clock, I was soothed by the sight and sound of the *aarati*—fiery candelabras swirling on the water of the Ganges accompanied by a prayer that was chanted to the divine river. I was rejuvenated by listening to discourses on Advaita Vedanta every afternoon. Meeting like-minded people with whom I could talk about miracles, life, and death gave me joy, fuel, and hope. Inevitably, supported by the deep devotion of the community that surrounded me, a path began to appear—one that had been clearly laid by the feet of feminine wisdom.

It was as if the time had come in my spiritual journey to reclaim the feminine universe and its orientation toward self-healing, transformation, and deep care for the invisible in us. From the beginning of my practice and especially when I lived in the monastery, I practiced like I was training to be a samurai. I followed a rigorous approach to meditation: If there was meant to be stillness, I stood still like a buddha statue. If there was silence to be maintained, I didn't open my mouth for any reason whatsoever (and was annoyed and irritated by anyone who did). I took the issue of awakening with the utmost seriousness, and when I heard other women evaluating the approach of Buddhism or Vipassana as being "too masculine," I judged that they were getting lost in petty arguments. I would hear nuns complaining about the lack of equality between them and the monks, and I would think, "Who cares! There's no time to worry about these conditioned things. We are here to wake up, girls, come on!"

I had always been comfortable with men. In the past, I often preferred to rely on men rather than women for support—even men I didn't know. I have generally found men to be sweet and nonjudgmental. I've never felt inferior or less capable around them; on the contrary, I often felt better seen, less interpreted, and more loved within my friendships with men. Of course, I did not realize that, in most cases, this was because they were attracted to me. Unaware of the dynamic, I took advantage of it. In the monastery, I perceived no difference between myself and my beloved Dharma brothers. Once I left the monastery, I pushed on proudly and determinedly until, thanks to a profound and revealing love story, I crashed into the trauma of the feminine. Frozen into form like an iceberg, it was stealthily waiting below the surface. This impact with an unseen and largely submerged reality helped me see how I had torpedoed and sunk the feminine to the bottom of my internal sea. A new sense of femininity arose, influencing my practice in unimagined ways. I found myself bewildered. Within me existed an extraordinary sensitivity and a bruised vulnerability. I found myself holding in my hands a forgotten and trembling feminine universe willing to shine through me, but I had no understanding of how that might happen.

Without warning and without explanation, God the Father became the Divine Mother. For the first time in my life, I was thirsty for sisters and fellow female seekers. Women began to interest me more than men, and female friendships became a precious part of my life in new and growing ways. At the same time, my relationships with men changed. I realized my dynamic with them had not been so innocent, and I stopped systematically and subtly using the power of seduction for the sake of receiving favors or the confirmation that I was beautiful and accepted in this world.

During those months in Rishikesh, I felt immense joy every time I met a woman searching for something unknown. I was drawn to the easeful surrender with which women allowed themselves to be led by their hearts. I was awed by the flame in their eyes and their burning enthusiasm for life. I reverenced those who were busy tidying the house because the Divine was coming to visit.

Women stirred a boundless tenderness in me. A woman inquiring into her true nature doesn't know what she is doing in any intellectual sense. She isn't following any particular rules or protocols. She is feeling and trusting her way into it because there is nothing left to do but that. She follows her heart carefully, shy and strong, humble and wild. With sometimes uncertain and other times unshakable courage, she questions the root of everything and is prepared to lose the world she has inhabited for so long. But as she turns toward the unknown, she finds herself surrounded by support, amid a storm of signs that tell her to keep going. None of this was known to me before, as if I had been disconnected from the collective side of our female nature. I felt I was walking alone in life, but then it became clear that we are walking together and that many women are walking in the direction of truth, love, and growth. When a woman dares to look into herself, the world opens up within her. Women in search of the truth unleash the beauty of life itself. They no longer belong to anything or anyone. They become powerful conduits of energy, like giant spools of electric wire, sources of illumination as graceful as fireflies, and vessels of profound depths echoing the mystery of deep canyons.

In this feminine sharing, I found a real remedy. I rediscovered the beauty of women and realized that I had never noticed it before. Bathing with my sisters in the Ganges, shimmering like half-dressed mermaids and singing Sanskrit songs to the river, I felt such love. We laughed like madwomen along the lanes and shared with each other the depths to which no words had ever been given. Infinite synchronicities resounded through each of our lives and bound us together. We each felt as if we were being embroidered by life into a luminous tapestry. I observed the beautiful way in which certain women dealt with grief, letting it melt completely into them to remold and reshape them. I learned that pain can be a force that reforms us, that we can become skilled at being reborn from ourselves at great speed. We can let ourselves die in surrender, if the time has come to let go of a part of us. We can and will reinvent ourselves with versatile creativity. The feminine universe enchanted me with its intricate complexity and its Shakti—the creative power that gives rise to the infinite forms we see.

Humbled by the Great Flood and gifted with the capacity of clearly perceiving sisterhood, I wanted to understand more about how to live my life as a perpetual encounter with the inexplicable love of the Divine. My understanding and perspective were newly unfolding, and I wondered what other women might be able to share with me, especially those who had walked a committed spiritual path. With a feeling of joy in my heart, I focused the little energy I had at that time on finding and interviewing these women, beginning an interfaith discourse on feminine self-knowledge and love that continues today.

Let us acknowledge that women have a distinctive way of dialoguing with the soul, and they have often done so without making a case for it or voicing it, narrating accounts of their spiritual intimacy through life itself instead. They have often embodied devotion without being noticed or acknowledged for it. The time has come to raise the voices of this distinctly feminine spirituality that runs close to the ground, so it can ignite a movement of openhearted contagion. It is time to make it clear and accessible—to bring to light the ability to cross sacred thresholds that lie within each of us and the capacity to use to our advantage the sensitivity and vulnerability that inhabit us. This is our noblest feminine power.

It can be frightening when a woman plunges into the mystery. Fear not! Mothers will not disappear; wives will not dissolve into nothingness. But we must learn to be there for ourselves if we hope to continue to be there for others. We tend to give a lot while forgetting ourselves, but we cannot function in life if we do not have time for our souls. Our daily nourishment comes from touching the diamond that lies deep within our hearts—something infinitely precious and brilliant, the priceless carat of being. If we turn inward, we find a garden that only our attention can access. There, we can engage in the care that reassembles the fragments of our soul. It is precisely in that deepest of intimacies that we discover that nothing is private, that the garden is not ours—it belongs to something far greater than us of which we are a part. It is precisely in that enveloping recollection that we experience openness and taste our invincible fullness. Only in this way will we frequent the garden of life with clarity of vision. Only in this way can life become a continuous finding of ourselves in everything.

Thanks to the demanding pressures of the ruthless society in which we live, we are witnessing the rise of an eager urgency to regain wholeness. We are crashing into icebergs only to melt into the ocean of self. Facing constant challenges on every front, it is as if the times are channeling us toward the recognition of our innate completeness, paradoxically saving us from getting trapped in new, more sophisticated, and intriguing fantasies about who we are.

As I searched to learn what I didn't know about women's wisdom, asking questions and gathering the answers became my path to wholeness. Women from a wide range of spiritual traditions, who have been walking the path for a long time, generously offered their guidance and insights, and the Women Awakening Project was born.

This book, a selection of my reflections on conversations with twelve of the many teachers I have spoken with, is a living room of worlds collapsing and worlds emerging. It is a source of guidance from Buddhist, Taoist, Hindu, Christian, Muslim, Jewish, and Nondual teachers who share their discoveries, their wounds, their talents, and their remedies for surviving pain and navigating life. I met them all in person while traveling in India, Italy, and the United States, and I thank them immensely for sharing their voices and their wisdom. They each contribute a vision that, woven together with the others, begins to create an invisible rescue net for us all, reversing the narrative of violence into one of liberation, awakening, and self-discovery amid an inner storm. Here, they show us how to tap into the impersonal power that enables us to face any challenge.

This project is a lively and open discourse that does not want to arrive at any conclusions. But emerging from the discourse, as if it exists just below the surface of the water, we can see the hint of a map of the inner territory. With your finger you can follow the faint trails of the suggested paths—paths that lead to the promised land, to the boundless dwelling that lies at the heart of awareness. For each of you, dear reader, the journey through this wisdom will unfold differently.

In this book, I speak of the feminine and the masculine, of women and men, sometimes in ways that may echo more traditional or archetypal understandings. My intention is never to exclude but to explore the inner and sacred dimensions of these energies as they manifest in all human beings. I ask for your understanding where the language may fall short of fully reflecting the rich spectrum of gender identities and experiences. Some approaches may seem to contradict others; there are perspectives that converge and others that drift apart. I hope you will take all of this into your heart because the path of mystery asks us to set aside our preferences, our need to understand. It asks us to welcome contradictions outside and within ourselves, to embrace the feeling of being unmoored. In the knowing of the heart, everything is in its rightful place. All that exists has a place in the grand unfolding. There is a hidden harmony—not buried, merely unseen—to which you can entrust your innermost feelings. May every reader feel welcome here, and find within these pages something true, tender, and resonant.

I invite you to leave the judging mind here, at the threshold. And if it still visits you as you read, simply notice it, accept it, and let it go. If something in the book does not make sense, it is the result of my inability to understand it fully, partially, or at all.

PART ONE

# Spark

## DISCOVERING THE DIVINE

The women we will meet in this book have devoted their lives to the Divine, yet they have also found ways to bridge the sacred and the secular. We begin by honoring those who have walked the path of renunciation, using the force of their commitment to spark their own inquiry. Four powerful voices, spanning from the Himalayas to New York, China, and Italy, are interwoven in a dialogue that answers many questions and, perhaps more importantly, raises new ones.

The first four interviews bring together the luminous wisdom of Jetsunma Tenzin Palmo, a Tibetan Buddhist nun; the sharp investigative spirit of Ayya Soma, a revolutionary Theravada Buddhist monastic; the contemplative depth of Antonietta Potente, a Christian nun who teaches the art of waiting; and the radical gentleness of Karine Martin, a Taoist priestess who redefines softness as strength. These four women stepped away from the world to embrace what is unseen, and they offer us profound treasures that will echo throughout our journey.

We begin with Jetsunma Tenzin Palmo, who was the only nun practicing among five hundred Tibetan monks until she withdrew to a cave for twelve years of solitary practice. Upon emerging from this experience, she built a monastery to provide a space for Himalayan nuns who did not yet have one. She didn't simply seek liberation for herself; she created the conditions for others to follow. And she vowed to attain liberation in a female body.

Next is a conversation with Ayya Soma, the first woman to establish a gender-inclusive Buddhist monastery where nuns and monks are treated as equals, defying the deeply ingrained structures of her own tradition.

Jetsunma Tenzin Palmo and Ayya Soma model not just acts of defiance but acts of belonging so deep that they have the power to reshape the very traditions they cherish. Their voices do not speak from the distant past; they speak from the present moment, rooted in lived experience. They force us to confront an urgent reality: In many spiritual traditions today, women are still met with systemic barriers. This resistance is precisely what fuels their compassionate action—the kind that ensures future generations of women will have the same opportunities for practice and support that monks have long taken for granted.

This is what high spirituality looks like when it turns into action. It acknowledges the emptiness of the world yet moves through it with purpose, tending to suffering and injustice where it appears. These women prove that obstacles can be transformed into strengths, that new structures can be created. As we read their words and gain clarity from their insights, we begin to see what it truly takes to do this: deep inner alignment, unwavering vision, and the courage to bring the Divine fully into the material world.

We turn next to Antonietta Potente, a Dominican theologian and fierce advocate for women's rights, who spent twenty years in Bolivia, standing on the front lines of wars over water and learning that true spirituality rises from the grassroots. And we meet Karine Martin, a French neuroscientist whose mystical experience in China led her to monastic life, where she spent twelve years in Taoist temples. From these two women we learn how to become receptive to the Divine and to remember that the greatest force in the universe is soft.

This is the revolution that calls us. A revolution of the West embracing the East, of the inner world embracing the outer, of serenity embracing and transforming adversity—a revolution that aims at calling us back to primordial bliss.

1

# Wisdom Is Feminine

## JETSUNMA TENZIN PALMO

In Buddhism, wisdom is feminine, like Sofia is.
We should appreciate the intuitive intelligence of
women and not try to model ourselves after paradigms
that are already proving to be a threat to the world.
We must support each other with joy.

—JETSUNMA TENZIN PALMO

Jetsunma Tenzin Palmo is a Buddhist nun in the Drukpa lineage of the Tibetan Kagyu tradition. In 1964, at the age of nineteen, she sailed from London to Dalhousie, in Himachal Pradesh, India, to pursue her spiritual quest. There she lived with Freda Bedi in a Tibetan refugee camp until, on her twenty-first birthday, she met her guru, Khamtrul Rinpoche, and was among the first Westerners to be ordained as a nun in the Tibetan tradition. She spent the years from age thirty-three to forty-five in a retreat in a Himalayan cave, surviving merciless winters (the cave was blocked by snow), extreme solitude, and the silence of the high mountains. At the end of the retreat, her guru gave her a new task: to start a nunnery for women from the Himalayan regions who often live in conditions adverse to practice. Jetsunma, who was recognized and loved for her accomplishments, began to travel the world, passing on wisdom and raising funds until she was able to establish the Dongyu Gatsal Ling Nunnery, or the DGL.

I traveled to this incredible nunnery, where more than one hundred Tibetan nuns live in uninterrupted practice and study. The DGL is in the Kangra Valley of northern India, surrounded by expanses of wheat fields and populated by a few houses with small flower gardens and chalk mandalas on their front doors. In the center of the DGL stands a temple with gilded doors from which strings of Tibetan flags radiate. While there are many female deities in Tibetan Buddhism, it is more common to see beautiful male-bodied buddhas, so it is a relief to walk through a place where the female figures are the center of attention, their images towering across the entire ten-foot-high temple wall. As often happens to me when I reach a place of worship or a place removed from the world, feelings of misery start to float to the surface, as if something disturbed an ocean floor, dislodging debris from the depths. As I take in the beauty of the place and feel the joy of anticipating my meeting with Jetsunma, I am also accompanied by a vague sense of nausea and a concrete awareness of the anguish that inhabits me. Under the rain, I run from my room to our meeting.

Jetsunma herself opens the door for me. After twelve years in retreat in a Himalayan cave, she vowed to achieve enlightenment in a female body, almost as a political statement. I became interested in her when I read *Cave in the Snow* by Vicki MacKenzie. The book recounts Jetsunma's retreat experience from which emerged Jetsunma's simple, pointed, and perfectly landed spirituality.

In person, as in photographs, she is incredibly sharp. She emits a light of great brilliance, her blue eyes are as piercing and honest as the brightest rivers of the highest mountains, and I had been warned that, if she wants to, she can read minds.

Being in her presence gives one the immediate confidence that the path of awakening is a tangible reality. We are in what seems to be a large, shining cave, with warm tones and lifelike Tibetan *thangkas* and a luminosity that seems to come from the way Jetsunma herself inhabits the space. I offer her my white *khata* (the traditional ceremonial scarf used to collect blessings) and a shy bow. We sit on a sofa and, with reverential awe, I ask her the first question:

***As women, how can we stand up in the world today in such a way that we are centered in love instead of anger, vindication, or competition?***

"Women must support each other, help each other, and avoid any antagonism, both toward each other and toward men," replies the venerable Jetsunma. She explains how this is exactly the spirit of the DGL. The nuns are mostly girls who support each other and live in harmony with each other. At the same time, they get along well with their "Dharma brothers," the monks of the nearby Tashi Jong monastery. The monks have passed on the knowledge of the Tibetan tradition to the nuns, and the nuns are very grateful for this. They have integrated it, assimilated it, and carried it forward. Now they are masters of their own destiny and no longer need to rely on the monks. But friendship and mutual support remain.

"Generating antagonism toward others adds no value to us," Jetsunma says.

I saw the nuns yesterday in the courtyard—about fifty girls with shaved heads, burgundy dresses, and open faces practicing debate, clapping their hands, and vigorously spouting arguments in the Tibetan language. Closing my eyes, I felt like I was at a municipal swimming pool in my hometown in Italy on a Saturday afternoon in July, the clapping of hands as loud as the impact of a young body diving into the water. The air was crisp and glowed with the afternoon sun. The girls' laughter echoed with the constant, exalted energy of youth. This morning, I heard them chanting the five o'clock Tara Puja and playing the *damaru*, the Tibetan drums that are sure to wake you up if you arrive at practice still a little sleepy. The girls joke and giggle as girls do anywhere in the world. They tease and pinch each other while they study the art of direct knowledge and the deep philosophy of being from morning to evening. They memorize practices and seek to internalize divine attributes. Their attitude toward the few female visitors who pass through, like me, alternates between a noble shyness and a shameless curiosity.

"It is very important that women do not try to model themselves after men, that they appreciate the richness of being a woman and all the qualities of the heart and the intelligence," Jetsunma continues. "In Buddhism, wisdom is feminine, like Sofia is. We should appreciate the intuitive intelligence of women and not try to model ourselves after paradigms that are already proving to be a threat to the world. We must support each other with joy."

She tells me about the Sakyadhita International Association of Buddhist Women, an organization entirely dedicated to women but in which enthusiastic men participate to a small extent. "It is very profeminist but not anti-male," she explains to me. At the organization's biannual reunion, monks, husbands, and male volunteers also come to help, and together everyone creates a truly joyful, celebratory atmosphere. "This is what women can bring to the world—a joyful festivity devoid of aggression, including celebration among women."

We hear a stream of rather discordant Indian music coming from the neighborhood. At this time of the day, according to Jetsunma, it can only be a wedding.

"I hope the woman likes her husband," she comments, with a broad smile. We take a few sips of our chai in pretty cups bearing Tibetan motifs. I am acutely aware and self-conscious of my every gesture and wish I could be more relaxed. I have absolutely no reason to be tense—apart from the fact that Jetsunma may be reading my mind. What could go wrong with that?

*How do you define the sacred feminine?*

"The sacred feminine is the essential quality of warmth and wisdom of the mind," Jetsunma answers. "[Male] teachers of meditation have told me that their best students are women because women are naturally at home with intuition, which makes them more inclined to meditation. In meditation, where men advance step-by-step, women can jump. They can jump and fly. This is innate in women, along with the warmth of emotions, given that they are so attuned to love, compassion, and the fundamental ability to nurture and care. After all, women are the ones who will raise the children. So naturally, they have a familiarity with contacting the heart without fear.

"In contrast, many men have been brought up in a way that they feel challenged by the connection to their heart—they do not know what to do with it. They mainly inhabit the rational brain, the part of the brain that makes them feel safe, while women feel perfectly at home in a landscape that is much more emotional. That warmth of clear intelligence, together with openness of heart, is what women should be proud of. They do not have to follow the male standard. We should generate our own path and be proud of it, without feeling that we owe someone an apology for it."

Jetsunma and I reflect on how, in many places in the world, the situation for women has improved significantly. In the past, women did not have the same opportunities as men and grew up believing that dependence on a male figure was necessary. It is sometimes men who are more dependent on women and not the other way around. It often happens that if a man loses his woman, he no longer knows what to do or how to take care of himself. Women, on the other hand, know how to take care of themselves. Their culture may still hem them in in some way, but the innate knowledge is there.

I have come to understand that to cultivate the feminine, we can connect to the natural reservoir of heart-mind qualities that already exists within us for the purpose of creating and maintaining life.

We innately carry empathy toward other beings' emotions and bear feelings of compassion, love, caring, and nurturing. We do not have to learn these things; they are already there because these are the ingredients of caring that help to create the sense and atmosphere of family, of home.

"Like Prajnaparamita, the Perfection of Wisdom," says Jetsunma. "She is voluptuous and feminine, but she is totally complete in herself. She is the summit of wisdom, the clear and deep insight into the nature of reality. The wisdom of emptiness."

In the temple, I notice a golden painting of Prajnaparamita, also known as Yum Chenmo, the Great Mother. She is considered the mother of all buddhas because it is from wisdom that buddhas are born. To take the flight of awakening, we need two wings: wisdom and compassion. Wisdom has the crucial role of severing the root of fundamental ignorance that keeps us bound to samsara, the cycle of death and rebirth. In this nunnery in the shadow of the Himalayas, I only now note that this wisdom, embodied as one of the most important entities on the Buddhist path, is in feminine form.

"Another example," Jetsunma continues, "is found in yoga tantra, where the male is always seen in union with the female, but females (in the various aspects of Shakti) can stand alone—they do not need the male. I believe this is also true in life. Women do just fine on their own, without a male counterpart. If they have one, fine; otherwise, they are perfectly capable of managing on their own."

At this point, I ask Jetsunma about Tara, the radiant savior. She enthusiastically replies that Tara stands for fearless compassion: "She is a strong lady. So nonjudgmental! She has tremendous compassion for us all. Whether we are good or bad on a relative level, she does not care. She sees into our hearts and treats each one of us as her own son or daughter."

While we typically petition male deities in an effort to capture the father's love, female deities are like the mothers of freely offered, unconditional love. "They reach out to us," Jetsunma says. "They come toward us, whereas with male deities we have to climb, climb up. Tara is always there for us. No matter what we do or how much we practice or do not practice, Tara is absolutely on our side, ready to intervene immediately as soon as we call her. That is why even for so many men, for example Atisha, the main deity is Tara—because she is so nonjudgmental and, at the same time, completely accessible. We do not have to be great practitioners to access Tara; she is there for everyone. Like a mother." Indeed, Tara is typically represented with her left leg outstretched and her right leg bent, symbolizing her readiness to rush in to help whenever needed.

We discuss another example of the power of the divine feminine—Vajrayogini—who is associated with *tummo*, the practice made famous by monks who can raise their body temperature so high they can dry wet blankets draped across their shoulders in the cold.

Jetsunma informs me that in yoga tantra, "man visualizes himself as a naked female." I imagine a very serious yogi seated in the lotus position with eyes closed, visualizing himself as Vajrayogini, the queen of the *dakinis*, and it strikes me as so unusual I nearly laugh! Among the different aspects she takes on is that of a red female deity. Depicted in fiery scarlet tones, she drinks the blood that symbolizes her experience of bliss. She represents pure inner fire and life force. And she is certainly not without curves: She has two beautiful, perfectly round and generous breasts, a very narrow waist, sensual hips, and long, wild hair.

Mind you, while the man visualizes himself as female, he does not do so to generate sexual energy and then transform it. He *is* Vajrayogini. We are living in a time when man must also become feminine to access a higher state of completeness.

As Jetsunma describes it, "Men's sexuality spills outward, so the big challenge for them is to reverse the flow of energy and bring it upward. In the case of women, this energy already goes upward; their sexuality is already inner, not outer. These practices are ideal for the female body and are easier for women. All books on the subject are written by men for other men, so many of these points are left out. The contribution of the feminine in this area is underestimated because it is of no interest to men to know that women are better than them in these practices. But if you look at it from a female point of view, you can see that in so many ways the female body and mind contain a great advantage. They are by no means a hindrance. If women have the opportunity to study or practice, they actually have an advantage."

Jetsunma tells me of a video she remembers seeing once. It was filmed in Tibet, in winter, in a snow-covered landscape. A line of hundreds of nuns, half naked, can be glimpsed walking toward a body of water in the mountains. They wear small white bras and carry a white sheet over their shoulders. They dip the sheet into the icy water, wrap it around their bare skin, and walk back the way they came. In the dead of winter, in Tibet, half naked, with wet sheets on! If the nuns were not experts in tummo, they would certainly freeze to death in that climate.

"In Tibet, there are certainly great female practitioners who are invited to teach the *kempo*, the monks, certain yogic practices and postures because they are the experts," Jetsunma says.

I remain silent. I am a little stunned by Jetsunma's presence, and for a moment, I am absorbed by the image of those admirable, half naked women, drying sheets in the snow with psychic heat. I think of those of us who use tumble dryers and wonder at all the women living lives perpendicular to my own. In the West, we are at a special moment in time. Women have conquered something; we are now in positions in the workplace that were unthinkable even just fifty years ago. But we have lost the ability to deeply contact our feminine side and its resources.

"Of course, you see, if women take the male model as an example, they simply become more aggressive," Jetsunma tells me. "Or they become Playboy bunnies and everything revolves around being pretty, feminine, and attractive. But they have lost the connection with the divine feminine, which is what they should be about! They are either absolutely trivial or too hard. They don't find a balance because they have no examples. They look around for examples, and they find curiosities about celebrities—who is fitter and what is fashionable to wear—or there is the model of the businesswoman who has a very masculine, aggressive, and tough orientation." But there is also a different, more feminine way of doing business, she asserts, and illustrates this claim with the following story.

Recently, one of India's greatest businessmen left his business to his wife when he died, which is very unusual in India. The son was so angry that he took the mother to court, but the wife won, and she decided to conduct the business in a different way—in "a women's way." Instead of sitting behind a desk and issuing directives, she took a collaborative approach, encouraging group decision-making and holding meetings within a circle instead of with a single person at the front of the room.

Here was a much more welcoming idea of doing business. In fact, the company has grown thanks to this approach. Jetsunma says, "This is following the divine feminine. It is about being inclusive, rather than about being a boss. But we lack models like these. Most books on how to succeed in business are written by men, and they do not promote an alternative way of relating to people—an egalitarian way that appreciates people and does not just treat them like attack dogs.

"A lot of women do not like to work for other women because they find it harder to deal with them. Somewhere we got it wrong, and I think that is because there is not much out there that explains how to do it the right way. As a woman, if you get into a leadership role, you get there by fighting three times harder than a man. You had to be smarter; you had to be better; you had to be more of everything, and that is bound to make a person tough, defensive, and aggressive."

In general, most of us have a preference for male authority figures because we are used to them. And a male boss is generally feared less than a female boss, with a few exceptions. Jetsunma says, "In India, there is a saying that when a girl gets married, the person she has to fear most is not her husband, but her mother-in-law."

Jetsunma goes on to explain, "Women's worst enemies are themselves. That is why we try to instill in the nuns self-confidence and respect for each other. Only in this way do we live in a harmonious family. Their potential is infinite, their limit is the sky, but they must support and help each other, and they do. Women must learn to appreciate their inner gifts without trying to become like men. We already have enough male energy in the world; we do not need more. What we need is a balance. But women have lost the understanding of what they want to achieve, which is a shame."

Reflecting on the harm we have done to each other as women and the suffering both men and women have caused each other, I decided to ask about healing these wounds in us in relation to the practice.

***From a Buddhist perspective, how do we deal with unresolved wounds and emotional blocks?***

"Buddhism is not psychiatry, but we must remember what the Buddha originally taught," Jetsunma stresses. "The teachings are not just about calming and taming the mad monkey mind. The other thing he said is that we should all, at first, do the meditations of loving-kindness, compassion, and joy, starting with ourselves. I think this is very important. Buddhism may seem to be mostly about fighting the ego, about nonself, about emptiness, but the Buddha said in the beginning, 'Become friends with yourself, because it is your ego that will have to walk the path.' To be able to do that—and then to develop deep understandings—we must be friends with our ego." This is a crucial point that I, and many spiritual seekers, lose sight of. I am happy that Jetsunma expresses it unequivocally, in such simple words: "Be friends with our ego."

"We must forgive ourselves, love ourselves, wish ourselves happiness; in other words, we must have a small, happy, healthy sense of self that will walk the path of nonself," she explains. "Otherwise, our self will not be able to walk on the path. If we break our leg, we cannot walk. All we do is to think about how much it hurts. As soon as someone touches us, we feel pain. And that leg is quite useless because it is broken. But when the leg heals, we can jump; we can run. We no longer think about our leg because it is healthy. So, when our ego is sick, we are constantly thinking, *I, I, I . . . poor me, I am so stupid, hopeless, I am too this, too that,* but it is just I, I, I. Instead, when we have a strong and healthy sense of self, when we are friends with ourselves, we do not think so much about ourselves, and we are much more interested in others. We are healthy and free from self-obsession. The problem with some of these psychological approaches is that we end up in the spiral of ego. In many cases, it can be easier to sit down and become friends with yourself instead of going into the spiral of solving every trauma. Forgive yourself and say, *It's OK.* Smile at yourself, and love yourself in a friendly way. Then you will be dealing with a happy little monkey."

Immediately, I wonder if my monkey is happy or not. It sticks its tongue out at me. Meditating with this monkey is sometimes a real struggle. I ask myself, *How can I let this go?* I ask the monkey to disappear into the trees because I absolutely must see the light beyond the blanket of forest in which the monkey holds me and entertains me.

"When we embrace that monkey, it will make the journey and transform into a buddha," says Jetsunma.

Here is the missing link in the chain, Darwin! The loving acceptance of the monkey so that the liberation of the mind is induced and spontaneous at the same time—not a forcing, not a compulsion.

"When we look at our mind, there should be no judgment," Jetsunma continues. "When we look at our thoughts, we are not commenting, *This is a good thought; this is a stupid thought.* It is just a thought. The same goes for emotions. Let go, let go, stop grasping. Thoughts and emotions are empty. In the true sense of the word—like bubbles. Very clear, very bright, but in a snap of the fingers they are gone. Or like a rainbow—they are formed by moisture, by the sun, by space. But you cannot grasp the rainbow. The Buddhist approach is to be in this state of openness and acceptance, rather than going into detailed analysis of what happened when I was three years old when my dad did this or that."

***That would be an infinite process.***

"Exactly, endless," Jetsunma says. "Rather, it is about recognizing that all these thoughts, emotions, memories, and ideas are just thoughts, emotions, memories, and ideas. They are not mine; they are not me. It is like watching a movie—a rather repetitive one, by the way."

Samuele Bersani's song "Replay" comes to mind. It is about being inside the continuous replay of a film that we project, in which we are the protagonists. Jetsunma continues with another effective and accessible image: "At some point, we recognize that we have to go beyond these repetitive patterns. We struggle because we have these neuronal pathways, like six-lane highways, that are easier to navigate the more they are traveled. But once we recognize that those six-lane highways lead nowhere, then we start to chart a different path. And that takes time and practice. But sooner or later, that new path will become a real road and grass will start to grow on the six-lane highway."

***Is awareness the key?***

"Yes," Jetsunma confirms. "Through awareness we can recognize that we are not these thoughts and emotions. There are thoughts and emotions that come and go, come and go. We do not try to stop them, but we stop identifying with them. They are like waves on the surface. That is the gross mind. The subtle mind is the ability to know and witness what is happening without being involved. With that awareness comes a certain degree of freedom. It is not ultimate freedom, because it is still something dualistic—there is an observer and something being observed—but behind that is the very subtle mind that is beyond duality and is the interconnectedness of all things: Everything is pure awareness.

"But to get to that state and stabilize in that recognition of pure awareness, we must first achieve dual awareness. Then, we sit by the river and watch the river flowing instead of being submerged and swept away by it. So, work on cultivating awareness. Observe the breath as a handhold. The point is not the breath itself; the point is the knowing—observing 'that which knows.' It is the quality of the mind that knows that we are trying to recognize and cultivate. And you can take that with you anywhere, not just when you sit in meditation, but all the time: that inner quality of very spacious and open presence.

"The fundamental Dharma is very simple. It is about becoming more aware, more clear, and cultivating a good heart. Then, one thing follows another. What we are trying to do is to be aware of mindfulness. It is always there, but we do not normally notice it. When it is cultivated enough, you feel the beauty of the inner poise; the mind is mostly flexible, clear, and open. If you hear a noise or experience an emotion that is difficult to take in, you are not disturbed or distracted by it because no matter what appears in the mind, you are with the knowing. You are in a boat and the waves no longer roll over you."

Thinking about how many times I have fallen out of the boat despite my efforts at practice and the many retreats I have done—or of the tidal waves formed in my sea—my face crumples. I feel in me all the granite solidity of a disgruntled ego, a geology of attachment to every micro thing I have felt was mine to own.

"Keep a big smile in your heart," Jetsunma tells me, sharing a radiant smile that immediately pacifies me. And in that moment, more than anything else, I am struck again by her sensational lightness, which feels like an ultimate revelation coming from inaccessible depths. This woman *knows* emptiness. She is mostly made of space, yet she is empathetic in a subtle, spherical way. If Jetsunma is a soap bubble, I am a solid bar of soap. Only repeated caresses of water can transform me. Only patience and persistence. A shower of gentleness and compassion falls on me. I finally let go. I relax, and the inner drama dissolves. The pillars of my inner structures melt a little bit.

Indian music is still playing out on the streets, and our time is running short. The venerable Jetsunma glances at the tray of fruit I brought as an offering, with its drooping bouquet of unknown flowers I had picked in the fields in a last-minute panic that my gift wasn't enough.

"Is that a mango?" she asks. And when I nod, she exclaims, "It is the first mango of the season! One good thing about May is that it is mango season."

I step out into the air scented by morning rain. The light reflects off the golden inlays of the temple. I walk around it, as tradition dictates, reciting a mantra, amazed at how incredibly fast the changes of mind are and at how contagious a calm mind and a peaceful heart can be. This is what happens when you start from the peak. As if I had climbed the Himalayas, thanks to Jetsunma, I now have a bird's-eye view of the situation. What do women today truly need? What is essential? Suddenly, the picture from above is crystal clear. A pantheon of female deities is available not only for inspiration but also for connecting with and activating forces and powers that are within us. We need female role models in spiritual life—women who showcase the potential for such inner empowerment—as well as healthy ones in the business world, in the realm of daily life. Women's intelligence is a treasure; we shall honor our intuition, and our only limit shall be the sky. We can achieve higher goals within ourselves, with love and grace, supporting one another. We can't lose touch with our hearts while gaining the greatest achievements in the world.

The way, though, is not so clear. Contemplating the highest mountains in the world, in an air so pure and alive, I wonder how we can truly embody that. To integrate this immense potential of women's wisdom in a healthy way—without losing ourselves in mere claims or personal or collective validation—we must cultivate a clarity as exceptional as the strikingly clear, pure, and crisp air atop the highest mountain peaks.

We need lucidity to navigate this realm of the spiritual feminine, to discern which battles are truly worth fighting and how to wage them wisely—with both intelligence and heart—without losing ourselves in them and while keeping our spirit alive to create the change that truly matters, the change that is needed. We need to pour our heart, flesh, bones, and strength into it, all guided by our spirit. Otherwise, we fight for clichés, engaging in battles without having truly delved into the issues that matter to us.

Coming together through shared feelings alone is not enough. For the light of knowledge to shine, the flame of inquiry must first be ignited.

2

# Awakening Beyond Gender

## AYYA SOMA AND BHANTE SUDDHASO

Gender is dogma. We have to identify it for ourselves, both on the meditation cushion and by looking at our own experience. What does it mean to be a woman? What does it mean to be a man? And how do we behave based on these definitions?

—AYYA SOMA

I arrived at the Empty Cloud Monastery in New Jersey on a November evening. The monastery was completely dark, and for a moment, I feared I had come too late. Then, a light turned on, a young monk opened the door, and I found myself in a serene realm of harmony, orchids, and translucent buddha statues. I met Ayya Soma in Italy, in Acquaviva, Puglia. She is a nun of the Theravada Buddhist tradition, the tradition that was my gateway into spirituality. I have profound love and respect for this tradition, and I can still remember how I felt, at the age of twenty-two, when I first arrived at the Theravada Buddhist monastery in the countryside of Rieti. It was like touching the ground for the first time in my whole life, as though I had to swim through deep waters just to arrive at that shore. I was safe. Here was the Dhamma, finally. (*Dhamma* is the same as the Sanskrit *Dharma*, but according to the tradition, the Pali word or the Sanskrit word is used interchangeably.) Here were the monks—reasonable people who were taking life seriously and graciously—meditating all day, which made total sense to me. I immediately fell in love with the whole monastic vibe. I would only meet the nuns later, when my own spiritual quest got more and more urgent.

Ayya Soma is a *bhikkhuni*, a fully ordained nun—a title that is difficult to obtain. This special ordination has sparked, and continues to spark, great controversy and division within the Theravada Buddhist world.

When I met Ayya Soma and the monk Bhante Suddhaso in Italy, I could hardly believe my eyes. A nun (bhikkhuni) and a monk (*bhikkhu*) working side by side within this tradition is truly rare, progressive, and groundbreaking. And when they told me about the gender-inclusive monastery they had founded in 2019 just outside New York, I promised myself I would see it with my own eyes. I wished to speak with them both to learn what they are doing together and to understand how men within spiritual traditions can be supportive of women's journeys.

Ayya Soma is a joyful woman in love with the Dhamma. She wears the classic robes in the color of burnt leaves and shaves her head. We sit in the beautiful meditation hall. Bhante Suddhaso, bright-eyed and composed, is sitting at her side and between them a huge bronze buddha offers blessings.

***What is it like to be a bhikkhuni? What's the story behind your ordination?***

"My story is slightly unusual," Ayya Soma replies. "I started a Buddhist organization as a laywoman with a bhikkhu, Bhante Suddhaso.

My interest, at the very beginning, was not to be ordained but simply to practice the Dhamma and be close to the monastics. At the time, I was living in New York City, and it was a bit complicated to gain access to monastics who could teach the Dhamma on a regular basis without having to travel for many hours. I met Bhante Suddhaso at the Bhavana Society in West Virginia, and he agreed to move to New York City for a period of time to share the Dhamma there. We opened a meditation center, and since we did not charge anything, I basically put my life on hold.

"I used to work as a freelancer back then, but I started living as a renunciant once we started this organization. I was working a lot to provide all these programs. My practice deepened, for renunciation is the core of Buddhist practice. As a result, I gained a deep taste for it. Soon after, I shaved my hair and realized I was not attached to it (though I had other attachments, of course). One day, I looked in the mirror and thought, *I look like a monk, I practice like a monk, and I live in a monastery.* Before coming across Buddhism, I was already looking for a way to make my life meaningful. But the fashion industry, the main sector I was working for, provided very few answers. I was looking for alternatives in the field of art and creativity, and that created the conditions for me to embark on a spiritual quest. By living like a renunciant and practicing, I had become happier than I had ever been in this life. It felt more like I was acknowledging that the monastic path was right for me rather than making a radical decision.

"I took my vows with venerable Pannavati—an African American bhikkhuni based in the US—who was my mentor and teacher in association with Bhante Suddhaso. After a couple of years, Bhante and I founded the Empty Cloud Monastery with the specific intention of starting a gender-inclusive monastery. This emerged from one of the paradoxical issues we find in Buddhism. We are supposed to transcend all our identities and attachments, and one of the main concepts is *anatta* (nonself)—the lack of a single pinpointed identity that I can call 'me,' 'myself,' or 'mine.' The teaching of anatta is basically what defines Buddhism, and the realization of anatta in every single aspect of our lives is what creates the conditions for liberation to happen. However, paradoxically, as soon as I entered the Buddhist world—coming from a fashion industry where gender was not really a major issue—I started noticing, for the first time, the fact that I was a woman. Before this, I had never really identified too much with being a woman, for many other identities had been at the forefront of my life.

"I found that in Buddhist environments there is a lot of emphasis on gender and on gendering people, and that certain implications and ideas are placed upon people who have specific bodies. This was very challenging for me in the beginning. Usually, as women, we are encouraged to endure all of this, and the teachings of anatta are used sometimes to have us internalize these sexist ideas. So, I saw my mind generating thoughts that were not helpful. For the first time, I found myself thinking, *I am not sure if I am capable of attaining awakening because I am a woman*. Prior to this, I had never had such thoughts in my life as, *I don't know if I can be an artist because I am a woman*, or *I don't know if I can be a manager because I am a woman*. The 'because I am a woman' piece had never been part of my way of thinking before my Buddhist practice, so I recognized it as a problem. I recollected the teachings of the Buddha in the *Sabbasava Sutta*, where he tells us that there is not just one way to deal with the *asavas*—the contaminations of the mind. He does not say that we have to endure everything. Instead, he says that we can avoid certain things that are not beneficial to our practice. So, in conversation with Bhante Suddhaso, we realized how unskillful this attitude is for everybody and wondered how we could create a space where gender is not the foremost problem."

I can't help but remember my time in the Buddhist monastery in England, when I was considering becoming a nun. I was glad to be there to immerse myself in the practice, and I still look at that time as one of the most precious of my life. But between the meditation sessions and the Dhamma talks, there were jokes about how unlucky it was that I was a woman because I couldn't walk the path like a man. I heard phrases like, "for women it is harder to completely let go of all the attachments" and "pray to be reborn as a man." The group of nuns I witnessed was not particularly happy. They were not unhappy because they were not practicing the Dhamma, the teaching of the Buddha, but because they were part of a not-at-all-Dhammic system—all they could do was swallow their protest and accept the status quo and transcend it, go beyond. Half of them had disrobed just a few years before. There was a pulsating wound in the body of the female sangha (group of monastics).

***What was the perspective on gender during the time of the Buddha?***

"In the earliest texts of the Pali Canon," Ayya Soma says, "we do not find this issue of gender. In fact, I get my name from bhikkhuni Soma, whose story illustrates this point. Bhikkhuni Soma is meditating in the forest when Mara (Lord of the senses) comes up to her and tries to instill doubts into her mind by asking her what she is doing there. A woman with little wisdom, what does she think she can achieve? She turns around, recognizes Mara immediately, and replies, 'What does womanhood have to do at all with awakening, when the mind is concentrated well and sees the Dhamma?' Also, in the instructions the Buddha gave to bhikkhus and bhikkhunis, gender is never mentioned. This gender neurosis and gender segregation was not there."

The Dhamma, the collection of the Buddha's teachings, is timeless but in every age, we are confronted with the conditionings of our time. How can we skillfully apply these timeless teachings to the present? From what I have observed, there is a lot of talk about gender in our society but not much direct investigation into it—not even in the Buddhist world, where the conditioning around gender inequality perpetuates itself.

"Gender is very interesting," Ayya Soma continues. "If we look at the animal realm, for example at cats, it is very difficult to differentiate between male and female. We have foxes in the monastery, which some refer to as she and others as he, but we have no idea which is which. With the majority of animals (unless they have distinctive marks) there is only a very subtle distinction of gender based on the genitalia and that's it.

"Because they are distant from us, the main characteristic that stands out in our mind is the species. But when we come to our own species, we find a very strong identity, and we see the subtleties more keenly. For example, we have very precise and specific ideas about what it means to be an Italian woman. Or we have very specific ideas about what it means to be a Westerner versus an Easterner, and so on. There are many things that arise in the context of gender, which are not universal. We take them to be universal, but they are not. There is not one universal way of being a woman. There is not one universal way of being a man.

"Certain things that are accepted in Italy for a woman are completely unacceptable in American society. And this is what the Buddha talks about in terms of emptiness: Everything dependently arises from many causes and conditions, which together generate a result that we take to be real.

"If we live in one environment, we will take on the conditions of that environment and build our identity around it—we won't question it. We think we are free to make choices, but we are not; we are acting in accordance with these constructions of realities. The teachings of the Buddha encourage us to question everything. That is the work that we need to do. We need to understand this process of how we fabricate our reality. The Buddha was not only ahead of his time twenty-five hundred years ago, he was also ahead of our time. We think we are so advanced, but we are not. There is a lot of talk about gender identification: 'I identify with this gender or that gender or no gender altogether,' but actually the Buddha pointed to the emptiness of gender and to transcending gender altogether. I would say that someone who has questioned gender to begin with—folks who have identified with the opposite gender or have a fluidity of gender—are already in a better place compared to those who, instead, have identified with their gender without ever questioning it since birth. The invitation of the Buddha is to see how we create gender and to penetrate into the emptiness of it and throw it all behind us."

Surely, investigating gender is not part of the teachings imparted in Buddhist monasteries, at least not in the ones I have attended. Rather, there is a tendency to avoid placing importance on gender and to move beyond it. Excellent! However, this can only happen if behaviors and habits are aligned with this idea of being "above" gender. I believe that this practice of investigating gender could be very interesting. It would allow us to truly go beyond gender in reality, not just in theory, and finally embrace the discomfort that this topic inevitably raises.

***How can we practice this inquiry on gender identification in the way the Buddha taught?***

"By reflecting and contemplating on what gender is our experience of gender can shift significantly," Ayya Soma says. "This has nothing to do with what we normally call meditation practice, but it is a meditation nonetheless. The original term for meditation is *bhavana*, which means "cultivation of the mind." Whenever we are cultivating the mind, we are asking these questions to ourselves and there is no difference between this practice and the practice of doing *anatta sanna* meditation [the practice of discovering the absence of self]. Mahamudra, for example, in the Tibetan system, is a way to understand the emptiness of all the ideas that we have, wherein you are invited to ask yourself certain questions, like What color is the mind? Is the mind inside of my body or outside of my body? What shape is the mind? What gender is the mind? I'm adding this one, but it is a valid question.

"It is not necessarily the point to find an answer, but rather, to identify our dogmas. We tend to think that dogmas are outside, that institutions give us dogmas, but we come to this world full of dogmas. Gender is dogma. We have to identify it for ourselves, both on the meditation cushion and by looking at our own experience. What does it mean to be a woman? What does it mean to be a man? How do we behave based on these definitions? What if we were to behave differently?

"To discard the self, we need to first understand the self. We cannot realize anatta [the absence of a self, or nonself] unless we understand the *atta* [the felt perception of a self]. Who do I think I am? This is a good question. Once we see that, then we can start looking at how all these components are dependently arising. We can use the lenses of the three universal characteristics the Buddha taught: *dukkha* [unsatisfactoriness], *anicca* [impermanence], and anatta. And we can see how all these attachments create dukkha.

"As I mentioned, I started realizing the implications of being a woman when I entered religious life. Before that, I was completely oblivious to the sexism that I had grown up with. When one is ignorant of something, one keeps perpetuating the same actions and solidifying that ignorance. It becomes like an infrastructure, a big solid building! Once you start seeing it, you can get rid of it. The suffering is relieved because you no longer need the support you thought was so fundamental. You identify the *muri maestri*—the load-bearing walls—from the fake walls, and you stop personalizing things.

"Whenever we see the dukkha and the emptiness of something, the mind naturally turns away, becomes dispassionate, and drops it. It is not a mental thing; it's experiential. It is how it works. Sitting meditation is good—and we also have to cultivate the mind 24/7.

"When we talk about any women-related issue in Buddhism, we tend to think that it's just a women's problem. But really it creates impediments for everyone to attain full awakening. It's a bhikkhu problem, it's a bhikkhuni problem, and it's a layperson problem too. A gender problem is a genderless problem."

Working on this project about women in spirituality, I encounter all kinds of discouragement from people, both men and women. I was told that bringing attention to a problem only exacerbates it. I don't agree; it depends on the way the attention is brought to the topic. If attention is brought to a problem accompanied by anger and resentment, of course the problem gets bigger. But if it can be done with compassion, discernment, and love for the practice and truth, it's a different story. The attitude with which we look at something changes everything. It can be a liberating process.

Bhante Suddhaso, who has been sitting quietly and attentively, shares his perspective: "Any kind of identity is ultimately an obstacle for awakening. But also, how we create and apply social constructs that are centered on identity is something that can contribute to the problem. If we focus on it, we can understand it. And if we can understand it, we can transcend it. Whereas if we pretend the problem isn't there, it doesn't go away. It's like having a broken leg, and you're just walking around as if nothing happened. Your leg will not heal. In fact, it will get worse. In the same way, Buddhism has a broken leg and 90 percent of the Buddhist world is saying, 'Everything is fine, just keep going.' We can't just keep going. It is a gigantic problem, and I think it is one of the main reasons why awakening is so rare these days.

"At this point, it has been twenty-five hundred years since the Buddha gave his teachings, and those teachings have been distorted for two thousand or more of those years. As Ayya Soma was saying, this is one of the distortions: We don't find it in the oldest layers of Buddhist teaching, but it is something that was added within a few hundred years after the Buddha died. People started adding these sharp gender distinctions.

"As long as we have this firm belief in some kind of identity, that 'I am . . . ______' (and it doesn't matter at all what you put in the blank, whether it's 'a man,' 'a woman,' 'an Italian,' 'French,' 'smarter,' or 'short'), it will prevent us from realizing anatta. For example, in Sri Lanka the main monastic order is open only to people of the highest class, which is mind-blowing because if you see the Buddhist teaching, basically every other page is about the pointlessness of the class system. Every other page is the Buddha saying there is no distinction between people of the different castes. There is no such thing as a Brahmin; there are just people.

"We have to question ourselves; otherwise we just go with what we are used to. One practice I find very useful is to ask, *What do I think I am?* or *What do I think defines me?* You can make a list of things that define being a woman or being a man. And then ask, *Is this the description of every single woman in the entire world? Does every single woman in the entire world have this trait?* Probably not. What are the traits that all women in the entire world have in common? Eventually you'll wind up with only descriptions of physical biology. Nothing else. Nothing to do with the mind. And in Buddhism what are we concerned with? With the development and training of the mind.

"Your mind is not different from my mind. We have slightly different bodies, but who cares? It doesn't matter at all. You have dark eyes; I have light eyes. What's the big deal? When would that ever have anything to do with awakening? We get incredibly fixated on the shapes of people's bodies. Nowhere in the *sutta* did the Buddha say that the shape of the body affects the capacity to attain awakening. In fact, we see the exact opposite. It is important to call these things into question. Our practice will go only to a certain level, and everything beneath that level will be full of delusions. We need to go all the way down, into the deepest layers of the mind."

This makes so much sense that I wonder why all the monasteries aren't talking about it. The conversations I have heard are often uncomfortable, struggling with the duality of promoting the values of awakening, liberation, and realization while finding yourself within a not-so-enlightened system that is difficult to change. It takes courage to change a system. Many monks I spoke with see the inequity of the monastic system, but most of them do not concern themselves with the fact that the most senior nuns must stand behind the most junior monk. Their priority is awakening, and these issues seem political and irrelevant. Must a monk or a nun also become an activist nowadays? My answer is yes. I understand that this path is not for everyone, but it should be for many. The Buddha was a revolutionary—every awakened master is. Revolutionaries do not sleep within traditions; they transform them so that what they profess becomes visible, a reality for all. They update everyone else's understanding of reality. And you don't need to be enlightened for that—it's enough to want to see reality as it is. What Ayya Soma and Bhante Suddhaso are doing is a revolution in robes.

Ayya Soma says, "There are two more gender-inclusive monasteries like ours: One is in Australia and the other is in New Zealand."

"Actually," adds Bhante, "What is bizarre is that we are talking about it as if it's something far-out and weird, while it should be normal!"

This makes us laugh. There's something inherently amusing about discussing something that should be normal as if it were entirely extraordinary.

"When you read the ancient discourses," Bhante continues, "you get a picture of how life was at the time of the Buddha: groups of bhikkhus and bhikkhunis traveling and practicing together, living in the forests in groups or alone, going for an alms round, listening to teachings, having Dhamma discussions, teaching laypeople—there is this sense of being all together. Then you look at the way Buddhism developed over the subsequent two thousand years and it's something completely different. Now, instead of gender-mixed groups that wander and practice in the forest, we have gender-separated groups that stay in one place for the rest of their lives. It's almost a completely different picture. It's quite strange when you think about it.

"The Buddha was a wanderer. In the suttas, we don't see the Buddha saying women are to sit on the right and men on the left or men are to be in front and women in the back or men should dress in this way and women in that way or the men go first and the women last. This is just not to be found. Every single monk or nun is independent and self-governed. One's teacher plays the role of an advisor, not a lord and master. The form of decision-making that we see described in the early Vinaya, the Buddha's instructions to monks and nuns, is group decision-making. There is no power structure at all. There is not an abbot or an abbess. All decision-making is consensual. There is no centralized power."

So, what is there to fear in implementing a change toward inclusion and equality of gender? Is offering women the same opportunities so frightening? What catastrophe will occur? I believe that somehow we need to go through this with courage, an open heart, and wisdom. For me, Ayya Soma and Bhante Suddhaso are the embodiment of something I felt was needed but didn't see happening. But there you go. As utopian as it may seem, it is already happening. And even if it remains a minority compared to the mainstream, what does it matter? What matters is that it happens. In the broader discourse of women's spirituality, these small yet courageous movements bring light and truth. We will always practice, no matter what. We will always remain viscerally connected to the Absolute and the Divine. But if external conditions support us—if men and women have the maturity to face reality and the strength to transform it—is that not a step forward for everyone on the journey to recognizing that we are one single consciousness?

It's almost eleven o'clock in the morning, time for lunch. In this tradition, there is no eating after twelve o'clock. When I was in the monastery, one of my favorite events of the day was the blessing of the food, which was chanted in the Pali language. Monks and nuns can't cook, prepare food, or even pick fruit from a tree; they can only accept what is offered to them. In this way, eating itself becomes a reminder not to take anything for granted and that we depend on others in countless ways. We adjourn and find the kitchen flooded with laypeople offering trays of food, a sign of gratitude for receiving the gift of the Dhamma.

I spent a week in this monastery, savoring quietness and its consequences. I felt the ecstatic devotion of polishing a human-sized statue of Tara each morning, had a wondrous meeting with a deer in the garden who came to test the boundaries of the property, and enjoyed steaming bowls of fragrant Thai noodles. There was silence between everything, a vast ocean of silence. The kindness of those around me, the careful practice of never saying more than is needed. To rediscover how humans can live together in a way that supports the arising of the mind's wholesome qualities brings a kind of astonishment. Why are we not living like this all the time? With this level of care and attention? And what does it mean to be a woman? I'll sit for hours and hours, listening for an answer that I never heard before, knowing above all else we can truly be of great support to one another.

# 3

# Sacred Anticipation

## ANTONIETTA POTENTE

> Wisdom can come from above, but it can also come from below. . . . In any case, it never comes from you; it is given to you. It is always a gift that arrives. That is why you must always be expecting it, both in your relationships with people and in your contemplation.
>
> —ANTONIETTA POTENTE

At home in Italy, which is known for its incredible beauty, delicious food, and the long arm of patriarchy known as the Catholic Church, I asked four people who do not know each other to suggest an out-of-the-ordinary Christian nun for me to speak to about my questions. All four people gave me the same name. Sometimes it is easy to not have any doubt.

It is a scorching August afternoon in Turin, and the streets radiate heat as I make my way to meet Antonietta Potente near the Church of the Gran Madre. Standing in one of those shaded, silent, and seemingly inconsequential alleys that have an air of peace, I knock on the door of a Dominican convent. An elderly nun opens it and asks me to follow her. The simple austerity transports me back to the twentieth century—everything is slightly old (although not really old by Italian standards), crucifixes are visible at every turn, and there is a faint hint of incense in the air.

The nun accompanies me into a room with a table and two chairs and leaves me there without saying a word. In front of me is a painting of the Madonna and Child. I place my vintage sunglasses, which somehow match the feel of this place, on the wooden table and wait. In a few minutes, Antonietta Potente arrives sporting jeans, a white T-shirt, a jaunty haircut, and a mysterious smile. Is she a nun? Yes, but she prefers to call herself a theologian who is committed to women's rights and mysticism. I ask her why she does not wear the monastic robe.

"There have always been mystery-loving women," she replies. "All these superstructures came much later, and not by the will of women. Women followed the mystery everywhere, in every religion and religious philosophy. By now, this is a path that anyone can follow, no matter how they dress or who or where they are."

I tell Antonietta about my experience with Christianity before I found Buddhism. I was baptized, happily received my First Communion, and, somewhat reluctantly, my confirmation. In a purely formal sense, I was raised Christian, and now it felt to me like having once dwelled in a beautiful shell. My parents gave me the freedom to walk my spiritual path, and at first, I thought it might be in this tradition. In my early twenties, I lived for a few months in a Christian community. At confession one day, as I was explaining to the priest my torments in great detail, his reply was, "It's not so complicated. You just have to surrender yourself to God." He said it as if it were the easiest thing in the world to do. At that time, I was in the throes of considerable inner storms, literally wandering in the woods with restlessness. I did not know how to pray. I could not find the inner space for a prayer. There was not enough air inside of me for the brilliant candle that turns toward the Divine to be lit.

Coming to Buddhism had been a great blessing, precisely because there was no believing or praying to be done. I found inner space thanks to the meditation practice and, together with it, a sense of awe for the Divine started to spontaneously grow. It seemed to me very astute to advance along the path of direct experience, and I have spent many hours in Buddhist and Hindu circles. But my roots lie in Christianity, and I would like to recover at least a more authentic and free sense of this persistent spiritual path, especially from the feminine perspective. I know there is also a great treasure to be found here.

"Among women, spirituality has been lived and told for centuries. But it has not attracted much attention," says Antonietta. "Women's spirituality has either been badly told, covered up, or immediately interpreted. The formation of the 'cloister' arrived very late in the structure of religious life. It is very clear that Clare of Assisi did not want the cloister, but today we know the Poor Clares to be cloistered nuns. In the eleventh century, there was no enclosure. There was male monasticism, but women were either nuns or lived together in lay communities called *beguinages*.

"Women who dedicate themselves to the mystery have always faced problems. Think of Marguerite Porete, the great mystic who was burnt and tortured. Even her writings were burnt, although fortunately some of them remain. In the 1300s, Catherine of Siena, a Dominican, was not a cloistered nun. She followed the way of the Mantellate—another form of beguinage—and dedicated much of her life to politics. I believe that women have always been close to the mystery, but in secret. Women have been overinterpreted and underheard. Today, many women are studying the ways of the women of the past, and beautiful things are coming to light that were not known. In the Bible as well, women were often spoken of by men. Today, it is we who must realize who they are and why they are important."

I admit my almost complete ignorance of the panorama of women's Christianity—with two exceptions. I offer my adoration to Saint

Clare whenever I am passing by the Porziuncola in Assisi, and Saint Teresa of Avila's book, *The Interior Castle*, left a lasting impression on me when I read it as a young girl. It describes the seven rooms of the castle that the soul passes through in its reunion with the Divine, and I thought it was actually a map to get to the hidden gem of life.

***I'm on this quest to understand more about the untold spirituality of women. How do women experience spirituality differently from men?***

"I believe women have a very different way of feeling," Antonietta answers. "In mysticism, feeling is very important, so there must be a difference. Men usually start from reasoning, whereas we arrive at reasoning through experience. That is why the mystical path suits women. I believe that our soul is also different. Women experience and express deep feelings differently. The relationship with mystery, for us, is very experiential. We may say the same thing in the end, but we arrive at it in a different way. In fact, we may not even say it in the same way. This is not only in Christianity but also in all other approaches."

A great effort to recover women's religious experiences has been underway since the late twentieth century. Antonietta brought my attention to a group that has still received little attention—the Desert Mothers. I have always been fascinated by the Desert Fathers—those men who, in the fifth century, followed the example of Jesus and left the city to go to live in the Egyptian desert as hermits. There, they dedicated themselves to a life of prayer and solitude. The deserts were the Himalayas of early Christianity—they are the lands upon which great realizations flourished. But I had not figured women into this scenario.

"There are female German authors," Antonietta continues, "who have done a lot of work in what used to be called patrology [the study of the early Church Fathers, or patristics] and that today, fortunately, at least in some areas, includes the study of the female tradition in

Christianity. Patristics refers to the first writings after the end of Christ's life, penned by those who had known Jesus of Nazareth. We always think of these writers as being male—as the Church Fathers. But books dedicated to the stories of women of that time have also been published recently. It turns out that there were not only men who lived the lives of hermits in the desert, but also women. Some went in search of liberation from their situation. For example, some were prostitutes. Others went because they were perhaps sisters of the Church Fathers. There was a time in the fourth century when many men and women lived as hermits in the desert. In some cases, they had spiritual relationships. Mostly they lived in caves, each on their own. Some of these women are mentioned in the books of the Church Fathers, and it is from those that we deduce their presence. We know of only a few anecdotes."

Suddenly, an image comes to mind: Women have always been there. I can almost *see* them. They were even in the desert, alongside the Fathers. Wherever there was a space for seeking or experiencing the mystery, there were women. What did they do? How did they fit into these contexts? They were there, yet no one questioned them. They were present, yet they sparked no interest and thus left no testimony. They carried on with their own work. History did not include them, but their experiences did not vanish into the wind. Even if they were not recorded in words, we can know that they were there—that behind us stretches an infinite garland of women who, wrapped in silence, uncovered the secrets of the inner world. Eager to hear about this new female ancestry being revealed to me, I asked for details.

***Who were these women? Can you share one of their stories?***

"Mary of Egypt, for example, was a prostitute," Antonietta replies. "It is known that she decided to embark on a penitential journey. She acquired the strength for it during a pilgrimage and decided to go to the desert. There, she lived alone until Zosimus, a desert monk, passed by and saw that there was a shadow in the cave. He called and called to her. In response, she said, 'I cannot go out because I am naked, and I am a woman.' He threw his cloak in her direction. Wearing it, she came out of the cave. From there, a friendship was born until one day he passed by and found her dead. Zosimus spoke of her as a virtuous woman, capable of living with very little. When he was about to bury her, it was difficult for him to dig because perhaps he was very old. A lion appeared and helped him—a classic sign of messianic peace, of the harmony this woman had created around her.

"Are these episodes true, or are they not true? It does not matter; someone narrated them. It's too little to go by as a reliable source, but one must never discard the dream, the popular narrative. The desert is not, as people think, just an escape from the world and from possessions. These are moralistic interpretations. The desert is a place of sensitivity, where the senses are sharpened."

What happens when we choose to cross the expanse and abide in this desert of our interior? I wonder. Is prayer the conduit?

***Does prayer naturally arise as a request for access to the more invisible world, as a plea for the unveiling of what would otherwise remain hidden from our sight?***

"The world of Christian prayer is very vast," Antonietta says. "The scriptures suggest it is a way to experience a familiarity with the mystery. There is the world of community prayer that is linked to the liturgy of the hours, the Psalms. And then there is a whole world of personal prayer, of a very direct experience of the mystery. I do not separate these much; they both seem important to me.

"To pray the Psalms is to pray with the words of others, alongside the history of a people. Perhaps the Psalms are a medium that brings you out of yourself so that you can feel that you are living inside of a story—a story of wars, injustices, and creation. Their themes are of building cities and their tales are of the righteous and the wicked.

But the Psalms also include more personal themes, especially the cry of longing. These examples help a lot. Each of us comes to prayer with our own experience, depending on where we are located within history, on our desires, anxieties, and worries, and on our wish to perceive how this human history is inhabited by mystery.

"This is the mystery: entering into a communication with the flow of a life that is more than our own. This seems to me to be the thing that makes us pray. In prayer, there is no need to say many things. Something always comes—people, words, or images—both in normal, everyday life and in the most solemn of moments. In my opinion, the most solemn prayer does not come on schedule. Prayer follows an expectation, but it means nothing if it is not accompanied by all this personal and constant waiting."

Being in a state of waiting as Antonietta describes it is a practice. Naturally, if we identify with the mind, the moment we start waiting, we are anticipating something incredible will happen. When will the angels appear to me? Will I have time to say goodbye to my loved ones, or will I go straight to paradise? What will it be like to meet God? But if we identify with the heart, which knows how to wait for itself at the threshold of the world, waiting becomes a process of ripening to receive grace.

***Sometimes I feel like praying, but I feel a tension, as if I am almost begging for an experience, a solution, an encounter with the Divine. Am I praying with the mind? What is the best attitude for prayer?***

"If one wants to understand something, it is normal to ask for help from the infinite," Antonietta responds. "Supplication is normal, especially for those who are living in very precarious situations or are suffering. Prayer depends on the image that each of us has of this mystery. Do I have the image of a patriarchal God who decides everything, or do I have an open image, a not-knowing? It is from here that the expectation and search are born.

"Sometimes, prayer is a constant search. It is listening, fine-tuning. It has many facets. My feeling is that the fewer the words, the better, but it all depends on the context. If a person cries out in blasphemy because he is nailed to a bed because he is unjustly in a prison, it is normal. The Hebrew scriptures make Job blaspheme for all the misfortunes that have befallen him. He has lost his children, his social position, everything. The pure ones try to console him, and he calls them the 'sickening comforters.'

"Prayer can be expressed in different ways and methods. The important thing is that it is true. If one looks a little at the history of prayer across religions and cultures, it is always linked to a context, to a sensibility. It is normal that the Tibetan monk or nun prays differently than we do because they come from another history, culture, and environment. Unfortunately, after the Vatican Council, which tried to modernize the church, the churches have become ugly. They make me sad. How can the people pray there? It is better to go outside, into the piazza. Or if one cannot, then one can sit on one's own terrace."

The ugliness of the church behind my house—a modern concrete hut—was, in fact, one of the reasons why, as a child, I couldn't believe in a God who lived inside it, as the catechists claimed. "This is the house of God," they would say. *How could He have created the world with its meadows, skies, and sunsets, only to choose to live in this concrete hut?* I would think. It didn't make any sense. I saw Him rather in the fields and waters, in the fireflies that inexplicably appeared in the evening in the forest. I thought that people had built the church to try to contain Him, like building a cage for a winged lion. Truly beautiful churches, on the other hand, have always given me the sense that they exist to honor what cannot be seen—something that surpasses even their own beauty. We associate God with the beauty of nature, which is ungraspable. And so, perhaps, our prayers, in order to encounter Him, must be somehow beautiful in the sense of being radically grounded and honest.

***How do we communicate to God the difficulties of our lives from a place of sincerity and beauty? If we desire to change something in our lives, does it make sense to include this desire in prayer, or should prayer be free of our own aspirations so we can truly make room for the Divine?***

"I do not advocate certain methods," Antonietta replies. "People can include a concrete desire for something in their prayer. If one asks for nonsense every day, I do not think it bothers anyone, but of course it's a waste of time. If you are real and you are there with all of yourself in those moments, then prayer becomes a rhythm. Christianity has mantras, which one repeats to oneself, keeps inside, and ruminates on.

"We live in the daily world and can't always stand with our wings raised, so prayer must be linked to life. It must be true. Union with life, through familiarity with the mystery, unfolds daily. In Christianity, prayer is expressed through the rite of the Eucharist, but it doesn't stop there. Prayer involves a total participation, even of the body. As Teresa of Avila used to say, 'Sit or stand, but be present.' The visions saints had during prayer shaped the very life they were living. Think of Saint Hildegard of Bingen, who had open-eyed visions. From a ray of light, she could understand many things.

"Other people's methods are interesting to know because they can help you on a path of research, but then you have to find your own way. You have to look a little deeper. We no longer live in A.D. 1000! Today there is no master, no real teacher who says everything, fortunately."

***It seems to me that finding one's own path is the path itself and through reaching "out" of the self to connect with something far greater, you also end up knowing yourself much better.***

"Religions do not come from above, they come from below, from human history, from human desire," says Antonietta. "Certainly, the spiritual quest coincides with a search for the self. Yours is different from mine and from anyone else's. Yet, I feel that the Divine also pulls you out of a self-centeredness and self-referentiality that can do harm over time. It is much better to open and make space for the Divine. Otherwise, it all becomes artificial. The greatest commandment found in Christianity is love. But if you are always focused on yourself, how can you love? The search makes you look beyond yourself. I believe that the wisdom of some Eastern experiences lies precisely in educating you to step out of self-centeredness. I think that is the beauty of Buddhism, for example. It is there also in Christian wisdom.

"Perhaps the height of heights is seen in humility. It is also grace because, in humility, one claims nothing. Very little is said about humility today. In the past, many treatises were written about it. I believe that a person, to enter a path of depth, must somehow recognize that the very fact of feeling—feeling at the level of the heart or soul—is a mystery. And so, one walks in a wake of humility, not expecting the whole world to lie at her feet or for everyone to do as she says. This path leads to a simpler, less complex life. Fortunately, life takes care of this for the person who seeks this profound intimacy.

"But you will never find anyone in writings or interviews saying, 'I am perfect; I am a master.' This is perhaps a more masculine approach—to want to be a guru. Women do not really care about that. We create life; we do not stand there and command life. We do not always need someone to come after us and obey us. My teachers—all these beautiful women—often are not even part of the religious sphere. Sometimes, they do not even speak. And that is fascinating, for it means that this path really is for everyone and for all. It is not for the elite. It is for a simple, pure heart, for those who search honestly, for those who perhaps do very ordinary things."

Without a doubt, the most extraordinary people are sometimes those who appear the most ordinary and unremarkable. I have met several women and men of this kind, where divinity is perfectly integrated into the human and there is no exceptional grandeur in appearance or manner. Sometimes, uncommon kindness, humility, and a constant joy accompany them in household tasks, work, and handling life's challenges. For when you find the safe harbor, you really can abide in an inner space of freedom from the happening. The realization of God is perhaps the realization of a constancy, the one true constant in this world. But for those who are searching—who have tasted the presence of the Divine but do not yet fully dwell in it—there are these dizzying oscillations between feeling and knowing that everything is grace and finding themselves as if abandoned in a cruel and often violent reality, where it becomes difficult to discern the imprint of God, which, nonetheless, must be there.

***Sometimes, life appears barren, and the Divine, especially the divine feminine, appears distant and unreachable. How do we cross this apparent absence of God?***

"In her book *The Mirror of Simple Souls*," Antonietta responds, "the mystic and beguine Marguerite Porete speaks of this as a situation of 'far-near.' I normally speak of it as 'presence-absence.' I believe that those who have gotten close to this profound quest, those who live with this tension toward the profound, also feel its absence. This tension can be felt in a very strong way in oneself but also in regard to history, for the violence present in our history—with its abandonment of beautiful things that are trampled on by humans—is precisely an absence. Presence and absence are not two separate things; they go together. Only those who experience presence can acknowledge absence. Or only those who experience, as Marguerite Porete would say, the near can perceive the far—the distance, the gap, something that is not yet here.

"I can no longer see the world divided into two—into black or white, into good or bad, into how this one is while the other is not. From self-centeredness, we want everything and always. But if we live in humility, simply, then it is normal that the experience of this depth sometimes becomes a great distance, or an emptiness and absence. I believe the Gospels also speak of this. I call this a state of nostalgia, but perhaps nostalgia is more about the past. One can be nostalgic for a very intense experience one has had or feel that something is missing. In Spanish, it would be *añorar*, or yearning.

"Maria Zambrano, a Spanish writer and philosopher, lived her life in exile for political reasons during the Spanish Civil War. We can perceive this yearning in her writings when she says, 'I love my exile.' When everything dear is taken away from us, there can be an epiphany, a realization of what's really there, nonetheless. A life dedicated to mystery is uncertain; it does not walk in security. It walks on the edge, through a fog, through the dark night. I do not see the dark night only as pain, but as the sharpening of the feeling that you are on a quest. You can wake up, as John of the Cross says, and set out onto this path, and it will seem to be dark because we are standing at the edge of our lives, where everything is not as clear."

I wonder if this perceived, yet unreal, distance from God serves as a way for us to let go of the final attachments before truly and solely embracing the Divine. War is one of those themes that is difficult to reconcile with the Divine. If nations arm themselves and stand ready for the worst, how can one see God in this? It is an old question. My answer now is that we cannot presume to know everything, to understand the mind of God or the reasons behind war. We must have faith that grace is always at work, most of the time in ways beyond our comprehension. Thus, all that we typically consider negative—war, violence, death—is, in truth, a manifestation of the same grace that grants us beauty, peace, and harmony with others. And this is the mystery we shall make peace with.

***You write in your book* Non calpestare l'ombra *(Do not step on the shadow): "Who divided the light from the shadow? The time has come not to step on the shadow." In what way can our shadow serve as a friend to our authentic quest? How can the shadow guide us?***

"Yes, once there is light, there is also shadow," Antonietta agrees. "And when it all seems like shadow to us because it is night, we can still experience light in the sense that we know that the sun has gone to sleep, or the moon might be present. I believe that our times are more night times than day times, but one really must realize that light and shadow are one. Does the shadow teach? Yes, it teaches. Sometimes, it makes you see in another way what light perhaps cannot show you. On the other hand, in light there is the happening of the midday, which is a precious hour because the two halves coincide. And where do they coincide? In you.

"I believe that we are called to grow toward unity rather than toward these separations we find so many instances of in academic language and in a certain type of science—a kind of ruthless rationalism that tends to separate everything. I wrote that book because one day I woke up and realized that light and shadow are the same thing: If there is no light, there is no shadow. The shadow always exists together with the light. Light's descent into the darkness is a great mystery. I believe that when we perceive that the light and shadow are one, then our senses awaken."

***You also wrote that "Life is an itinerary, an inner pilgrimage, a progressive approach to the mystery. Any doctrine that wants to unveil God is nothing but a small door. We would like to get to God through a sapiential approach." What do you mean by a "sapiential approach"?***

"A sapiential approach," Antonietta says, "is one that comes without our reasoning. Wisdom can come from above, but it can also come from below. I lived in Bolivia with indigenous Bolivian people, and it was there that I discovered that wisdom also comes from below. In any case, it never comes from you; it is given to you. It is always a gift that arrives. That is why you must always be expecting it, both in your relationships with people and in your contemplation.

"The sapiential approach takes away the great weight of this Western knowledge that is not knowledge but rather an accumulation of all the things one knows. Wisdom is not accumulated knowledge. But she who has accumulated knowledge can also be wise if she leaves room for that which is not hers and that which belongs to others—in other words, if she leaves room for the Divine. We would have to include wisdom in our science and theology, which is often so founded on dogma—as if dogma is the be-all and end-all of everything—while often taking away our desire to directly perceive that perhaps something is yet to come. And, if it comes, then this something comes from wisdom, which is feminine."

***Women have often been seen as keepers of faith, passing down beliefs through generations, embodying devotion, and playing crucial roles in religious and mystical experiences. Sometimes we talk of blind faith. How can we develop an awake devotion? What is the relationship between faith and inner vision?***

"Faith is about watching," Antonietta asserts. "In my opinion, you must be able to wait, watch, and listen. For me, these are the most useful verbs for living. I don't believe that faith is blind. It is intelligent, though sometimes it relies on a tradition and sometimes on the wisdom of others. We must always be waiting for life to speak to us. Maybe that is what faith is. It is not the attainment of certainties but the faith that life will speak, though we do not know when. Maybe it will speak to me when I reach one hundred years of age, if I reach one hundred years of age. Or maybe it will speak to me when I least expect it. But life does speak. So, what do I have to do? I have to be very awake to this reality. In the Book of Revelation, there are repeated refrains such as, 'I was looking and . . .' or 'I was looking and I heard behind me . . .' I think these are beautiful. Faith is just like these refrains. I am looking and then, what happens? We watch. This is faith.

"Faith also gives us the strength to continue on our path. The great annunciations happen to people who are waiting. The annunciation is not a conclusion, but a start to a new phase of this looking, this searching, this waiting. Faith is also a virtue, and virtues are attitudes of daily life. Trust in the mystery, and also in total surrender. Notice how the Muslims pray—with such great faith that even their bodies become like fetuses when they prostrate themselves on the ground the way that they do. It is really a religion of self-abandonment.

"I believe that life is made up of not only what I see, but also of so much more. So, I must surrender myself to that which is much more—to that which I do not know and yet search for every day."

Little did I know that, coming out of this interview, I would miss my train. Intoxicated by the spiritual elixir that Antonietta offered to me with her presence and words, I felt happily drunk. In my spiritually inebriated state, I wound up going north instead of south, only to realize this too late. Later that evening, I listened to an interview that Antonietta shared with me. It is the only interview ever made with the great teacher Cristina Campo, an Italian writer, poet, translator, and essayist known for her deeply refined and mystical approach to literature. Her books, especially *Gli imperdonabili* (The unforgivables), have, on the one hand, filled me with despair—her writing so precise and beautiful it is unattainable. On the other hand, they have given me immense inspiration, and her fascination with the sacred in everyday life has been a true source of nourishment for me. The interview could be considered complete after the very first question and answer in which Cristina feels perplexed about the interviewer's interest in her person.

The interviewer asks her, "Can't you talk about yourself?"

Cristina replies, "I hope I shall never know."

There is enormous space in allowing ourselves the freedom to wait for life to speak to us. The journey unfolds through both action and pause. The fullness lies in the energies and qualities we can invest, but at times, these take the form of emptiness—emptiness of action, emptiness of demand. They are good absences, like the absence of claims or the absence of the need for results. And those are truly our sacred spaces where we restore ourselves and recharge so that we can put forth effort in the skillful direction of our life while also knowing when and how to hold back—in other words, which spaces to leave empty.

Waiting as a sacred practice removes the notion of getting somewhere or achieving a goal and shifts the focus to the possibility of receiving, opening us to the intervention of grace, which is the only thing that really exists.

4

# The Strength of Softness

## KARINE MARTIN

> The Tao Te Ching teaches that softness is
> the most powerful force in the world.
>
> —KARINE MARTIN

In Rishikesh, India, when I began to recover from the pain caused by my vertebra and the all-pervasive suffering, I would go every day to listen to wisdom talks at an ashram focused on nonduality, or *Advaita Vedanta*. The term *Advaita* means "not two," emphasizing that there is no real separation between the individual self and the ultimate reality. Vedanta is a spiritual and philosophical tradition rooted in the end portion of the Vedas. This path recognizes the ultimate wisdom that there is only one undivided consciousness.

One evening, the ashram's swami, a monk in the Hindu tradition, invited Karine Martin, a Taoist priestess, to an interfaith dialogue. Radiating a background aura of silence, Karine captured the attention of everyone present. She was "cloud wandering," a Taoist term for having stepped away from everyday tasks and responsibilities to engage in spiritual travel or pilgrimage. An aptly poetic description as she herself emanated the softness of a passing cloud in the immensity of the sky with her billowing white clothes, blue shawl, gray curls gathered softly in an elegant, Asian-style high chignon, and her soothing spontaneity.

A few days after I heard her speak, Karine welcomed me into her room in Ram Jhula, the quietest area of Rishikesh, at the foot of the mountains on the northeast side of the city. A neuroscience researcher, Karine is also a Taoist nun and Quanzhen priestess. She has lived for more than fifteen years in Taoist temples in China and is the founder of the France-Tao organization in Montlucon, not far from Lyon.

Nothing in her feels tense, and there seems to be space for everything. Like a cloud that knows how intimately it belongs to the sky, she gives the impression of being a woman who makes room for the infinite possibility embedded in each moment.

Karine sits on one of those white plastic garden chairs that are so ubiquitous in India. I sit on her bed, next to a folded-up blanket made from some synthetic fiber that at first you dislike but then, inexplicably, grow fond of. The room is like many in India: The floor is cool and gleaming beneath bare feet, a wide window opens to a lush tangle of green, insects flit and shimmer at the edges of your vision, and the warm breeze teases the heavy curtains and creaky wooden doors.

I knew very little about Taoism. During crucial moments in my life, I had flipped through the Tao Te Ching hunting for answers, reading it with all the haste in the world and devouring its stanzas like shrimp cocktail at a Chinese restaurant. I know even less about the role of women in the Taoist tradition and am very surprised by what Karine tells me. This is possibly the first time I am meeting a nun who has no complaints about the religious system to which she belongs.

"In the Taoist path," she says, "there is an extraordinary equality between men and women. In the temple, we wear the same clothes, and women can perform functions and rituals and even be the abbess of an all-male monastery. No distinction is made between men and women. I think it is because Taoism is based on the notion of yin and yang, and one can't exist without the other."

Yin and yang form a symbol of the naturally balanced dynamism between opposites. It indicates the synthesis of the movement of all situations—mental and emotional states included. Within a young woman full of strength and beauty there is already the seed of old age and death. In the dead autumn leaves, there is already the sign of the spring to come. For yin becomes yang and yang becomes yin. In the heart of joy, sadness is also present. Just as in disgrace, grace is already there. A thin thread separates day and night, feminine and masculine, opening and closing, and so on, ad infinitum. These forces dwell in the same circle and share energetic space equally—to the point that one contains the principle of the other, thus calling it into being and becoming, into manifestation. Despite the popularity of the symbol, the secrets it holds still seem to elude us.

"One cannot exist without the other," Karine asserts. "Yin is not more important than yang, nor yang more important than yin. It is the interaction of the two that matters. It is a pair of opposites, and that is how the world works. In the Tao, you look at the masculine and the feminine with equanimity because that is the heart of Taoist philosophy. It is reflected in your way of life, including the way you run the temple and the way you teach disciples. How can you teach yin and yang and then consider the man superior to the woman or vice versa? In Taoist philosophy, the harmony of the world depends on yin and yang coexisting at the same level."

If I correctly understand this symbol and its profound meaning, opposites do not dissolve into each other; they alternate and balance each other continuously. One does not break through or make war on its opposite. It finds a way to be in harmony with it. There is no rivalry between day and night. Night does not want to last longer than day. The sun (often personified as male) gives way to the moon (a typically female symbol), and then the moon submits to the sun. Otherwise, every sunrise and sunset would be a war. Instead, precisely in those passing hours, there is perfect harmony and often stunning beauty in the transition. In the symbol of yin and yang, in the thin line dividing the white from the black, I sense an almost superior form of intelligence and respect, an order of nature that we humans tend to disrupt again and again in preference to our own tastes.

"In the Tao Te Ching, the foundational text of Taoist philosophy," Karine continues, "there are many references to feminine energy. It asks, 'Can you be like the female?' and associates the feminine with qualities like openness, softness, and gentleness, which are often symbolized by water. The Tao Te Ching teaches that softness is the most powerful force in the world. For example, a drop of water, if it falls on a stone in the same spot, continuously and gently, will wear away the stone. Instead of using strength and a hammer—and getting tired in the process—with time and regularity, gentleness and kindness, that drop of water that falls again and again on the same spot on the stone wears it away. This is the feminine quality."

***This image of the drop repeatedly but calmly falling on the stone, wearing it away, reminds me of the process of meditation.***

"Exactly," Karine agrees. "The wonderful thing about sacred texts is that they can be interpreted at various layers. The same sentence can have many meanings. Yes, this is one of the possible readings. In fact, in meditation we sit softly with receptivity, every day, at the same time, on our cushion. We do not push; we do not use strength. Instead, we bring our soft attention to our breath or body or to our mind. The observation done in this way, on a regular basis, will open the darkness, will wear away the stone, will let the light in. And then the awareness is just . . . there."

I am struck by Karine's softness and how this softness does not translate as loose or fragile. She is sharp and strong, neither like a downy chick nor a raging bull but rather like some middle creature—not a cross between opposites, just another being.

"In Taoism, we speak of meditation as an internal alchemy—a transformation of our energies, both mental and physical," she says. "Practices begin by developing yin—receptivity. Because once yin is present, then there is a spontaneous connection with nature—with qi, energy—and things can begin to move and transform. Many traditional texts and masters say a woman progresses faster in internal alchemy at first because she already has that yin quality developed within her more than men do. At some point, men and women progress in the same way, but initially women progress faster. Although this certainly does not mean that women are superior to men."

***How do we understand the feminine and masculine polarity that dwells in all of us—men and women alike? How do we discover one if it has become hidden or if it fell out of balance?***

"One of the first steps in the practice is to create harmony between yin and yang, so that they are present in the same quantity, so that they flow and interact with each other harmoniously," Karine replies. "They are inside of us: yin qualities and yang qualities. There are yin channels and yang channels, the meridians. There are yin aspects and yang aspects to each organ. This polarity is within us, and that harmony must be created within us. Then it will spread to the world, but it starts inside of us."

I ask her what practices can be done for this, imagining myself on the banks of the nearby Ganges attempting to balance yin and yang.

"Yes, there can be practices," she responds, "but I would like to say that there are specific practices for specific people. Taoism was not taught to a group of people—it was taught to one person. The teacher would interact with the disciple on a personal level. Depending on where the student was in their training, and based on his or her energetic constitution, mind, and so on, he or she would be given specific techniques. As the disciple progressed, the techniques changed. You cannot talk about a single technique to harmonize yin and yang because it depends on who you are. It is a very personalized way of teaching."

Practice is part of what I am seeking from these conversations. How can I practice differently if I don't learn different practices? Perhaps Karine sees the disappointment on my face, despite my attempt to hide it, because she offers me a place to begin.

"If we really wanted to find a general practice," she counsels, "it would be to observe within yourself one thing and its opposite. For example, to realize that there is anger and also gentleness inside you, and that one is not more important than the other. It is about making peace with all emotions. The moment you come to look with equanimity at an emotion that you consider to be negative, and then at one that you consider to be positive, then yin and yang are in harmony. This then becomes the ability to look at whatever arises in us with equanimity, whether it is a powerful yang anger or a very yin sadness. By looking at them with equanimity, you create balance."

As she speaks, I connect with the very yin sadness I have been feeling for the past few days. I feel a tenderness that I had not previously felt. When I am sad, I usually retreat to a point that is far from me, others, and the truth—a point where I stand feeling lonely and lost, like an exile deprived of any possibility of returning. What is missing in those moments? Awareness? Softness?

"One must develop the ability to be a neutral observer of what arises within, without judging it, classifying it, naming it, rejecting it, or grasping it," Karine continues. "Simply let it go, like a cloud passing through a valley. Do not try to grasp a cloud. The cloud will pass. Your emotions and your thoughts are like that. There is no point in saying 'this is good, this is bad.' They all have the same nature, which is to be an object created by the mind. They all come from the same source."

For a moment, her words lead me there—into the silence of absorption, when the mind is allowed to return to its own home, to the origin. What a relief! I slowly begin to recognize this simple truth that is already known by every cell in my body.

***What do you think of the focus on healing the feminine? I feel it's necessary, but at times it feels tricky. Surely, within us women, there are memories of generational pain, but at times, it feels like entering a tunnel with no end, where one takes on an identity of suffering that is, in truth, of no real use to spiritual evolution.***

"Yes, it is tricky because what is the feminine?" Karine asks. "Is it a status that society gives us? Is being feminine about being fluffy and kind, wearing pink dresses and makeup, and smiling? Or is it about being a woman with children who cooks for her husband? We have to be careful about this notion of the feminine. Is this not another conditioning—to think that being feminine is this and being masculine is that, and that we should therefore submit to this game, accept our roles, and behave accordingly?

"I think healing the feminine is more about healing yourself as a being. You are much more than feminine or masculine. You are a being. Once the being is healed, then the masculine and feminine are healed.

"We should look at our conditioning and detach ourselves from it so we can get closer to our true nature. It could be that I love wearing makeup, or that I do not like it, but that does not make me less feminine. Stay close to your genuine impulse and do not follow impulses that come from external conditioning, from the education you received, what you were told was right or wrong, or from the desire to be liked or loved. Follow the genuine impulse that comes from your true nature. And in the morning, spontaneously, you either put on makeup or you do not. There is no thought that says, 'If I do not wear makeup, I am not beautiful.'"

I love the idea that each of us should feel free to express our beauty in our own way, without the need to conform to certain standards.

There can be freedom in the manifestation. We can manifest ourselves however we choose. Some embrace their natural beauty, while others find joy in the ritual of tracing eyeliner along their eyes, adding volume to their lashes, or enhancing their lips. For example, in the monastery, makeup was, of course, not worn. After a year without it, I had grown unaccustomed to it, and wearing it started to seem like something "unspiritual" to do. If you are truly spiritual, you don't concern yourself with such details of appearance—at least, that's what I believed. But that thought came from a judgmental ego, and fortunately, I freed myself from it. Now, I have returned to wearing makeup and enjoy a bold eye.

***We know we are not just this body, but we can still appreciate it and celebrate it with a sense of freedom.***

"Yes, freedom," Karine agrees. "Be free. First, free your being and then you will see how your feminine expresses itself. It is like a flower. And maybe your feminine side will take on a pink or yellow color. You are a woman. Physically, we are women, we do not go against that fact. We live in a body that is feminine, and through it your nature will express itself. Allow your nature to manifest."

I like to hear that there is a consequentiality between tuning in to your core essence and the outer manifestation of it. I think about the emphasis on self-care and tending ourselves from the outside and wonder if it's a common misconception that this is the way to be our authentic selves.

***How important are self-love and self-care on the spiritual path? There is often a tendency to downplay the significance of this physical or relative self.***

"Self-love and self-care are already part of who we are," Karine says. "We are born with this love for ourselves. A child will never think or say, 'I hate myself.' The child is fully present in acting, doing, being. Before the external judgments come—you are behaving good/bad—the child is happy and smiling. That is self-love. That is pure presence. It is when we get out of the state of presence that thoughts such as 'I'm not good enough' or 'I'm not beautiful enough' come in. This happens when we give too much importance to what is said on the outside, and when our focus is on what people say or what TV or radio or advertisements say, for example. Instead of listening to our inner voice, we listen to external voices and lose our connection. Disconnection leads to hatred. When you are disconnected, you are unfulfilled. In that dissatisfaction, you don't feel love for yourself because trying to achieve happiness outside of yourself leads ultimately to constant dissatisfaction. But since the source of happiness is in love, and it starts from you, it is all about being grounded within."

It is impossible at this point not to ask about what self we are talking about. Who is this self we are trying to love? How does she/he/it relate to the true nature of who we are? Karine explains that, in the Tao, our true nature, or "real person," is called *Zhenren* and is thought to already be inside each of us, gestating like an embryo.

"Once you are in touch with that, with the Zhenren," she says, "then there is only self-love, because there is love for everything."

I want to ask how I can make an appointment with my Zhenren, this true being in my heart. If it is always here within me, it might be that I feel a distance because I moved away from it. In everyday life, we are looking for Zhenren—behind every face we encounter, behind every action and movement.

***How is it possible for a laywoman who is immersed in the world to keep up a sincere spiritual practice? How can we find our Zhenren and look to balance yin and yang amid everyday life?***

"I am deeply convinced that laywomen can reach the same level of achievement as nuns who devote their whole lives to it," Karine stresses. "I am absolutely convinced of that. My path, my karma, my dharma, was to practice in this way, as a nun. But practicing as a laywoman is also beautiful and maybe even more difficult because you have to be even more focused so that you do not get distracted by other activities. You have to make sure that you always have time for practice but also time for your family. It is a beautiful and difficult practice that will also lead you faster to high achievements. Moreover, because you have no choice but to apply the practice to every daily action, you will more quickly develop the ability to stay centered and aware no matter what happens."

Karine's spirit and generosity are heartening and encouraging. I sense that the spirituality expressed by women has an intrinsic softness and aspires to a freedom that is truly radical because it has had to embrace and transcend sociocultural norms. As active and engaged women, we must still be able to land within ourselves, in our heart, from which love first flows toward ourselves and then toward others and from which also arises the unique creativity to manifest ourselves in the way that resonates most deeply with us. If we wish to cultivate spirituality, it does not mean we must necessarily dress in a burlap sack to hide our curves (as I did a few years ago). Knowing who we are, we do not lose ourselves in the image of who we think we should be. In this sense, women's spirituality transcends even the myth of image and feminine beauty, which so often entrap us.

***Do you have any practical advice for implementing this in our daily lives?***

"No matter how busy you are, you should always set aside time just for you," Karine advises. "Even just ten minutes a day. You probably spend more than ten minutes during the day watching TV or having a cup of coffee with a friend. Make sure you keep ten minutes a day just for yourself in which to practice—to anchor yourself and remind yourself that you are on the path. Throughout the day, maintain a sense of body awareness in your actions. For example, where is my hand? Now I am talking to you, I am engaged in this interview, and I am very excited. But I know that my hand is here resting on the armrest of the chair, and my feet are on the floor. This keeps the awareness within, instead of going all over the place with the mind. So always be aware of what you are doing. This is a very important thing to do. Also, observe the breath. As you go grocery shopping, buy vegetables, whatever you do, notice it. Maybe you are not breathing freely. Relax your shoulders and let go.

"These little things are very important. I do not think that one can realize the Tao or go far in the practice if one only practices sitting meditation and then forgets it when she goes out. As our patriarch Lao-tzu teaches, meditation happens when you lie down, when you sit, when you walk, when you stand. It is in every action. Laywomen are in the ideal situation to put these teachings into practice. Imagine the energy women can bring to their children if they can approach mothering as a meditation—it would be good for the whole family. Of course, the partner feels it instantly, too. It is something that is immediately reflected in those around us. If the woman is relaxed, serene, and centered, it naturally brings balance back to the family, which we know is the basic building block of society. If you are tense, even if you do not say anything, your children will scream and fight. If you take a deep breath, relax your shoulders, and center yourself, you will see that their attitude changes too. They calm down. If there is less agitation inside you, there will be less agitation outside as well. It is very powerful.

"Women are quite stressed these days because they are trying to be too many things at the same time. Society says you have to be strong, a powerful businesswoman, a good mother and wife, and that brings confusion. It becomes difficult to manage all these roles. Simply be in tune with what you really want and follow that. The rest will happen by itself."

***I am particularly drawn to female deities. Is there any representation of the divine feminine in Taoism? What form does she take?***

"Women have always played an important role as deities, even creating some of the most important ancient schools," Karine tells me. "The Shangqing, or Highest Purity School, was created entirely by a woman, Wei Huacun, who became a goddess and, through the channel of mediumship, transmitted texts that now constitute one-third of the Taoist canon. The woman's role is also to transmit the Tao; that is, the practices to realize it.

"Then there are female deities who are an emanation of the Tao, such as Doumu, the mother of the stars or the mother of the constellations, who is the main deity of my temple in France. She gave birth to the stars, particularly the seven stars of the Big Dipper. But she is considered the mother of all stars, and therefore she is responsible for everything that shines in the sky, including the sun and the moon. Since she is the mother of the stars, she is also indirectly or directly responsible for the fate of mankind because fate is linked to the movements of the constellations. You cannot find a temple in China where Doumu is not present. She is normally surrounded by the sixty cycles in which time was traditionally measured, and everyone prays to her on their birthday. Even when we feel unlucky, we pray to her. On New Year's Day, we have big ceremonies for her. She is very important. She has eight arms—in her two upper hands she holds the sun and the moon, and in the other hands she holds objects of power to remove impurities and get rid of negative energies.

"In our school, the Complete Reality School, there is Sun Pu-erh, a married woman with children, who realized the Tao in the twelfth century. It is said that of seven disciples, it was she who reached the highest level of realization. Sun Pu-erh then left behind texts and practices especially aimed at women.

"There are a lot of other female deities, including Hou Tu, the empress of the earth; Xi Wang Mu, the queen mother of the West, who taught the Yellow Emperor, the mythological emperor of China from whom Chinese civilization was born; and Nuwa who created humans from earth.

"I have two female teachers whom I also want to acknowledge: One was Cao Ye, a hermit in Huashan, China. I bow to her and thank her because it is through her teachings and support that I was able to progress on the path. And then Wu Fanzang, the abbess of the Eternal Spring Temple, who took care of me. Maybe they arranged this meeting!"

I'm completely open to the possibility that, from above, a greater vision weaves together the threads of our lives in ways we could never imagine. In the perfect timing of the universe, it suddenly becomes clear that our meeting has come to an end—like a jar emptied of its contents. It is time to move on and integrate. The world returns, like a caravan of colors and sounds, inhabited by time, space, and other wild creatures. Karine walks me to the exit of the guesthouse. I ask her how long she will stay in Rishikesh.

"I have no idea! I decide day by day. I do not know what I am going to do tomorrow," she replies amusedly, with the wisdom of a sky that does not want to predict the weather.

This is how I travel now too. I occasionally accuse myself of extremism, yet it works. Life flows on its own. I did not—could not—plan to meet Karine. It just happened in a perfectly natural way, and meeting her gave me a clue about how to move forward. When embarking on a journey like this, you can't expect a clear formula with an easy solution. Balance a bit of yin, welcome yang more openly, and off you go—bloom into the world as an awakened woman.

This approach is much more than a method or a set of techniques. Maybe it isn't even an approach at all. Yet, the attitude in this subtle inquiry can—and perhaps must—be guided first and foremost by the quality of softness. This is not the kind of softness that leads many women to let things slide just to avoid confrontation, to pretend not to see in order to avoid change. Our greatest ally is the softness of the greatest force in the universe—that gentle, exquisite power that makes us capable of incredible resilience, endows us with a humility to receive the greatest gifts, and is flexible enough to dance with all the unexpected obstacles of life. This soft power is what enables us to change states while remaining aware that our nature is space itself.

In this cycle of forms that is a woman's body, in this great instrument, finding soft strength is not difficult. It's already within us. The challenging part is to make space for all the forms within us, as well as the formless. Karine's words remind us of the way forward: It's okay to wander, to drift like a cloud. The path doesn't have to be straight. We are allowed to wander.

PART TWO

# Gestation

## SURRENDERING TO THE DARKNESS

Once the spark is lit, as the first four conversations in this book modeled for us, combustion begins. And so, we turn inward. What do we see? A darkness that is vast, unmapped, and humming with everything we have yet to know about ourselves. It is the dark unknowing, the silent weight of what has been buried but also the womb of life itself. The blocks are deeply felt—rooted in places whose origins are lost to time, yet undeniably present. It takes rare courage to step toward this unknown, to stand before it without flinching. Here, the laws of light do not apply. Time stretches, and the boundary between life and death grows thin.

The women in part 2 show us how to navigate this terrain. Francesca Bocca-Aldaqre, an Italian theologian who embraced Islam, walks this precarious edge with knowledge and faith as her lantern. A scholar, theologian, and mother, she is carving a new way to speak of Islam in Italy, walking a path fraught with both peril and possibility, armed with intellect and devotion. Marina Borruso transforms nonduality from an abstract philosophy into an embodied experience, inviting us to step into the river of ourselves—the very current we have always feared would sweep us away. She reframes the darkness within not as an abyss but as a threshold to the Divine.

To enter this shadowed terrain—the realm of interiority, whose ultimate promise is to meet ourselves in the heart of light—some, like Paramjyoti Carola Stieber, dare to dance with its shadows. Trained in the sacred dance of the devadasis, she carries their lost gestures across continents, shaping them into forms that whisper to the modern soul. Others, like Elena Brower, lean into the presence of the dying to learn what it means to truly live. A mother, artist, poet, and teacher, Elena stands at the threshold where presence meets impermanence, weaving movement, stillness, and words into a profound practice of living.

These women are bold creatives, disciplined and irreverent guides. They do not turn away from the difficult, the weighty, or the unspoken. Instead, they step inside, each following her own alchemical path. They offer us startlingly practical remedies for those moments when we find ourselves stranded before the locked doors within.

Four paths, four flames, each illuminating the inevitable descent into the dark that comes when we step beyond the known. How do we shield ourselves? How do we move through density?

This is not just philosophy. It is not just thought. It is the body, the breath, the way we move through the world. Now, we turn to the flesh—to the meeting place of spirit and form. Here, the way we move through daily life and dwell in our bodies can unbind old chains, reveal the unseen, and ease the deepest fear of all: death. We can learn to embrace the darkness so fully that, when it manifests in our daily life, it finds us unafraid.

5

# The Wings of Faith

## FRANCESCA BOCCA-ALDAQRE

Hope and awareness are the two wings of faith.
On one side, there is hope, and on the other,
an awareness of the weight of one's mission.
If these wings are unbalanced, one cannot soar.

—FRANCESCA BOCCA-ALDAQRE

I knew very little about Islam when I set out to find a female imam or other spiritual leader to speak with me about her experience in what is often perceived as a religion particularly oppressive to women. Luckily, I had an Italian friend, Margherita, who had converted to Islam when she married a Muslim man. Whenever I am in Bergamo, the town of my birth, we meet and share with each other the joys and struggles of our respective spiritual paths. I admire her beautiful hijab, hear new words of Arabic slip from her tongue, and listen to her concerns, including her fear of the prejudice and misunderstanding that her mixed-race children encounter and how it is difficult to find female role models who are practicing an integrated spirituality that is suited to a modern world and a modern family like her own.

Why would a free Western woman, after all the battles fought for women's rights by her predecessors, embrace a religion that has a reputation for being restrictive and outdated, if not outright dangerous for women? Why would a woman who can dress however she pleases choose to adopt excessive modesty and cover herself with such rigor? As she listened to her spirit and followed the path of her personal spiritual journey, Margherita had to grapple with these questions and find answers herself. Much of this work was done on her own as she searched for someone to help her make sense of what her heart was telling her. Finally, she called me one day to tell me she had found the guide she was desperately looking for.

Italian-born Francesca Bocca-Aldaqre is a scholar, author, and counselor in Islamic studies and psychology. On a rainy yet bright day, Margherita and I set off from Bergamo to Piacenza to meet Francesca. She greets us at a gas station with a welcoming smile and guides us into the city's industrial zone where we make our way to a mosque hidden among the factory buildings.

Francesca is thirty-six years old and exudes a youthful yet timeless aura. She dresses with style: a loose plaid jacket over an elegant outfit. The mosque is empty and perfectly silent in the morning. In the hushed quiet of the sacred space, I ask her about her unusual journey.

***How did your interest in and love for the Muslim religion come into being? What was the reaction of your Italian family to this spiritual life choice?***

"It has been a long journey of discovering Islam and Arab culture, two distinct aspects that I came to know at different points in time," Francesca responds. "My very first encounter with this world happened when I was fourteen years old and read Goethe's *West-Eastern Divan*, a collection of poems where Goethe imagines conversing with figures from the Islamic, Persian, and Arab worlds. I was deeply intrigued because he depicted this world as serene and filled with dialogue, exchange, and what he called cultural traffic. For me, poetry has always been a primary channel for exploring the world. I have a deep love for poetry, especially poetry from places or times unfamiliar to me. That was where my interest began.

"Later, living in Piacenza, there were no Muslims or mosques at the time, so this interest remained purely theoretical until I moved to Germany for my studies. In Germany, I encountered a Muslim community, primarily of Turkish origin, now in their fourth or fifth generation. Meeting this community was a joyful experience, and it was there that I began to learn Arabic and sought to deepen my understanding, especially through travel. For me, traveling became a privileged way to observe and understand how Islam is lived and practiced.

"The reaction of my family and friends to my conversion was, overall, positive. People understood I was going through a profound journey of learning and exploration and that what was happening to me was part of a broader curiosity about the world around me. Additionally, I've never been a particularly conventional person, so my decision probably wasn't a huge surprise to those who knew me! They likely saw it as another step in my pursuit of intellectual and spiritual stimulation in less traditional spaces."

***People tend to have a negative view of Islam in the West, though I don't think they understand the depth and breadth of Islamic cultures and beliefs. What does Islam mean to you?***

"This is a really difficult question," Francesca says. "I believe one of the meanings of Islam is trusting surrender to the will of God. But this definition I've borrowed because it's the one Goethe gave in his personal letters when he was trying to explain to those around him what Islam was. I don't think there's a better way to express it in an Indo-European language. The challenge with Arabic is that every word has to be translated with a sentence—even people's names. If you ask an Arabic person what his or her name means, it's a sentence. And so, Islam is also a sentence. Unfortunately, the media is used to translating it as 'submission,' which is completely wrong, because 'to submit' is a transitive verb—to submit to someone—and there's a tremendous unspoken element in this translation that takes away the whole dynamic of the soul's surrender, which is truly what Islam is about. I believe 'trusting surrender' is a good translation."

I think to myself how much courage and perseverance it would take to uphold one's religious faith in a society that constantly misinterprets and criticizes it. To remain whole in such a pursuit would require a great inner flame and a deep commitment to tending and nurturing it.

***Have there been women, either within or outside of Islam, who have inspired you on your journey of exploration?***

"Yes, so many," Francesca replies. "The first environment where I encountered inspiring female figures was in Syria during my early travels in 2008. There, I had the honor of meeting many women active in teaching Islam, who lived and embodied it in a culturally elevated way within society. During that same period, I got married in Syria, and I had the example of my mother-in-law, Ada, who taught me the foundational ethical and moral aspects of Islam, which I believe are the most important. These teachings pertain to behavior and daily ethics. Islam is a religion that speaks deeply to the direction of our hearts in everyday actions, even in the most seemingly trivial matters, like speaking, cooking, or cleaning. This left one of the strongest impressions on me. Another key figure for me at that time in Syria was an aunt I gained through marriage—Faize. She has an incredible story. At one point, she was forced to flee Syria for religious reasons. She then lived a very humble life for many years in Jordan, and she showed me how one can live Islam even while having absolutely nothing. Her example left a profound impact on me.

"In Damascus, there were truly dozens of women worth mentioning, women I encountered when learning Arabic, the Quran, and other foundational teachings. All of them were exemplary figures. I pray that God protects them during these difficult times in Syria.

"Outside of Syria, I have encountered fewer women who could serve as role models, and that is because, unfortunately in Europe, a true class of Muslim female thinkers has yet to emerge. I've noticed that Muslim women in Europe tend to somewhat neglect the traditional sciences—studying the Quran, the Hadith, the *fiqh* [Islamic jurisprudence], and the primary sources of theology. While in Muslim countries there is a centuries-old tradition of women scholars; here there are almost none. As far as I know, none exist here in Italy.

"In Germany, however, one of the most important role models for me has been Annemarie Schimmel. She was a university professor and a genius. During the Nazi era, she learned Persian and escaped, traveling to Persia, India, and Turkey. She learned the languages of these regions and became a university professor there. Her spiritual journey was extraordinary. She worked extensively in the field of translation to bring Islamic thought into a form that was not simply a linguistic translation of what had already been written in Arabic, Persian, or Turkish but a true translation of thought. This is crucial because European thought is fundamentally different from Semitic thought.

"Another figure of reference for me, this time in the French-speaking world, is Eva Meirovitch. She was a great writer and translator who succeeded in shaping Islamic thought for a Francophone audience."

Perhaps precisely because of the lack of an adequate translation of Semitic thought, there exists a space—both socially and culturally—for the Arab culture and the Islamic religion to be misinterpreted. This difficulty that some spiritual traditions face in being seen in their authentic essence may be a necessary obscurity—one that compels us to make a deeper excavation into the divine message. Adversities on the spiritual path do not happen only to individuals but also to the traditions themselves. It is as if darkness—understood as ignorance of the self, lack of vision, inability to comprehend, distortion, and obscuration—is intrinsic to all things until we become the very light in which everything unfolds. Many women are bearers of light, illuminating difficult and misunderstood paths, restoring the simplicity of divine order. Just as the women Francesca mentioned have been a source of encouragement for her, I am certain that the subtle and wise work she is doing is already transforming the hearts of many Muslim women.

***Can a Western woman find freedom and elevation by embracing Islamic practices and its precepts? Certain daily practices—such as wearing the veil—are often perceived as a limit to personal freedom by those who don't understand the reasons behind these gestures. Can you explain how these precepts are not limiting, or if they are, in what way?***

"Thank you for framing the question this way," Francesca replies. "Usually, it is asked in quite a different manner. The answer to this is complex. I don't believe that everyone can find the same things in everything. What I find in Islam isn't necessarily what another convert might find or what another Western person might discover in it.

"From a theological perspective, we believe that God has given each person their own path and a specific way to experience things—not necessarily higher or lower, but a different mode of perception. I absolutely believe that it is possible to find a way of living Islam that is compatible with a sense of freedom, emancipation, and so on. However, for me, these are not the first priorities. What I seek in following Islamic precepts is fundamentally to draw closer to God—nothing more.

"But if you ask me whether I feel free, my answer is yes, totally free. That said, I don't believe we're talking about the same definition of freedom, and I think this is a field where communication becomes very difficult because we move from the realm of practiced religion to the realm of true mysticism, where the experience of the heart is very, very hard to convey.

"I have many friends who are converts and practicing Muslim women, and they tell me that emancipation is a crucial element of wearing the veil. For them, it's essential to show that they are Muslim in a society that may, in some ways, reject them. For other women, wearing the veil is a way of staying connected to their culture of origin and preserving the last traces of what it means to come from another land. And I believe all these experiences are valid."

***Your latest book,* Manifesto dell'Islam Italiano *(Manifesto of Italian Islam), debunks many myths about Islam. What are the most important myths you are trying to bust, and what is essential to understand about Islam today?***

"I am attempting to address the most pressing issues from an Islamic perspective—that is, from the point of view of a Muslim," says Francesca. "Among our most urgent concerns are how we are portrayed in the national media, the safety of mosques, and the Islamic heritage in Italy. For almost a thousand years, Muslims have lived and died on this peninsula, yet the Muslim footprint in Italy has been erased. In many places, like Venice or Sicily, there were houses, tombs, and mosques that have disappeared. We don't want to disappear. *Manifesto* is an attempt to say, 'We exist,' and to leave a trace.

"Another goal is to speak without being put on trial. I believe this is one of the most important myths to dispel. Muslims are almost solely included in the public discourse or dialogue when something bad happens, when it's time to condemn a terrorist act, a crime, or some obscenity. I'm often asked to appear on TV programs where I'm expected to play a role that enhances an underlying Islamophobia or racism. I am also trying to confront Islamic thought itself, which is currently in crisis. I want to have a conversation about change, both in the culture that receives it and in Islamic thought itself."

***Islam is often seen as intolerant toward other religions. Living in a multicultural country, how do you understand Islam's teachings on religious diversity?***

"We must not forget that Islam practiced in Muslim-majority countries is quite different from Islam lived as a minority, as it is here," Francesca warns. "Historically, Islam has demonstrated a capacity for coexistence that has yielded undeniable results. Think, for example, of Andalusia, Spain, with its centers of learning and a caliphate court made up of people from many different faiths. If we compare that to the representation of different faiths in our modern parliaments, for instance, I don't think we see the same inclusivity.

"Similarly, if we look at the Ottoman Empire—a long-standing example of Islam in practice—the organization of the state was distinctly different for Muslims and non-Muslims. Muslims were recognized as an independent community with their own laws and rules. This represents a model of coexistence and multiculturalism that we in the West struggle to conceive. In the framework of the nation-state, there is only one law for everyone. In Islam, however, each community is allowed its own laws.

"I believe this is a crucial potential strength in managing a multicultural society. In this way, Islam challenges many of our certainties about how we organize ourselves, how we view coexistence and plurality. It forces us to realize that perhaps the way we view pluralism isn't as pluralistic as we think it is."

I believe spirituality, understood as the science of being or the awareness of interconnectedness, is fundamentally rooted—regardless of the form it takes or the belief it adopts—in a core openness. This openness does not imply a blind inclusivity but rather a willingness to recognize the same seed of truth in what appears different. What could be more spiritual than embracing someone completely different from you, someone who believes in another God? That kind of openness is a true form of spirituality and fulfillment and a cause of peace. What could be more spiritual than making space for a minority? What could be more spiritual than really listening to a voice that has been distorted or neglected, such as the voices of women throughout history? And what if it were precisely their voices—the ones we have not heard—that carry the most valuable messages for our times?

Given that the dominant narratives so clearly shape the masses in a particular way, and we are now immersed in the catastrophic results of those influences, might it be that by making space for other messages—such as those of softness or of facing darkness with the right perspective of the heart—we could bring about results that are more grounded in compassion and love? It is my dream that the voices of women will flow like water, wherever they are needed, bringing clarity, healing, and wisdom.

***It seems like you have an important mission at the crossroads of Italian society, Arab culture, and the Muslim religion. What is your dream? What would you like to see come to fruition?***

"My dream," Francesca maintains, "is for the Muslim minority in Italy to breathe new life into Italian culture. To see young Muslims active in art, literature, and poetry and becoming an integral part of Italian cultural expression. Islam has always brought poetry, art, and beauty to every culture it has touched, yet the cultural contributions of Muslims in this sense have barely been explored in the West.

"Human beings fulfill their potential through spirituality, culture, art, beauty, environmental preservation, and many other fields. My dream is for our human contribution to be recognized. When faced with discrimination, we shift into defense mode, and defensiveness does not allow for creation. I hope we can reconnect with our creative roots and contribute to the creation of beauty in this world."

***Is it faith that helps you pursue such an important dream?***

"Hope and awareness are the two wings of faith," says Francesca. "On one side, there is hope, and on the other, an awareness of the weight of one's mission. If these wings are unbalanced, one cannot soar."

***Humanity is going through major global challenges. How do you think we can keep our faith, an open heart, and an inclusive attitude toward diversity amid all of this?***

"It is difficult," admits Francesca. "Keeping the heart open requires hard work. And today, it seems that the main enemy is precisely the resistance to doing this work, in any field. We live in a society driven by entertainment and distraction, and this is the first enemy we must fight with all means. Distraction leads to overconsumption, to the destruction of resources, as we try to console ourselves with material things for what is more accurately a nonmaterial need.

"There are urgent matters calling us to this work. You can see a clear difference when something is done with heart versus when it's not. Take, for example, the reaction to environmental regulations introduced by the European Parliament—how anger or frustration arises when people feel forced to consume less or produce fewer things that harm the environment. But if this effort came from a place of love for creation, it would be far easier to respect nature, seeing its beauty clearly. This is an important reflection for our times.

"Another way to preserve the openness of the heart is by maintaining connections with past and future generations. Edmund Burke, the Irish theologian, argued that a society functions well only when there is a covenant between the dead, the living, and the yet to be born. This covenant means that earlier generations strive to pass on to those living today things in their best form—a house built to last generations, for example—so that the current generation can preserve it, along with its environment and the animals around it, and pass it on in turn.

"This sense of continuity has been completely lost under capitalism, which drives us to overwork and to produce surplus for others, leaving no time to do the essential work on ourselves. To break free from this system and step off the hamster wheel, we must give up certain levels of luxury and privilege and the status symbols we hold so dear. Doing so allows the heart to open to the world.

"The dream this society offers us is one of production, environmental exploitation, and destruction. It leaves no room for openness of any kind. We must not let ourselves be deceived by advertisements, product placement, or media consumption that doesn't help us grow spiritually. We need to stop cultivating the unnecessary, because the unnecessary has a grip on our hearts."

With gratitude and a sense of intimacy, we conclude the interview, aware that the midday prayer is about to begin in the mosque. Stepping out into the pale white sky of Piacenza, we bid farewell to Francesca as if she were a long-lost sister. In Margherita's eyes, there is immense joy—she has found a wise ally, a valuable guide on her journey into the challenging sides of mystery.

My conversations with many of the teachers I speak with often start with women but quickly widen to include circles of men, children, society, cultures, and our global community. Women's spirituality is inexhaustible and touches every aspect of life. Surrendering to God is a personal practice but also a political act. Faith has real-world implications. Throughout history, spiritual surrender has fueled resistance movements. From Joan of Arc's defiance to Gandhi's nonviolent struggle against colonialism to the Civil Rights Movement, faith has been a force for justice. It also raises questions today: To whom or what do we surrender in daily life? Are we surrendering to a system that enslaves us more and more? What implicit agreements do we commit to?

Surrendering implies trust, devotion, and a shift in allegiance, often away from worldly systems of power and toward something higher. This can be deeply political because it challenges dominant ideologies, societal expectations, and even governmental authority. Spirituality does not necessarily have to carry this political connotation to be defined as such, but it can. As many moments in human history have proven, spirituality can change the world.

To change the state of things within us or around us, sometimes we must go into the darkness to find our soft strength—a strength that only the love for the Divine can provide. This sounds similar to the "trusting surrender to the will of God" that Francesca referred to: a surrender that increases our capacity to take a deeper look at ourselves and our shortcomings, making space for the peace that is present inside of us so we can bring it forward and offer it to the world. Courage and perseverance naturally arise when we find what's important to be preserved, protected, and nourished in our heart. We become able to face what we never faced before. We find we can encounter what once seemed unreachable and unapproachable within us. We realize we can meet darkness with open eyes.

Surrender is a vast and spacious invitation—a sacred place where we lay down our heaviest burdens and entrust them to what we call God. In surrender, we trust that we are seen and held by the most loving gaze. It is a profound calling; one we often answer when life presses us to the edge. In that moment, we realize we control nothing—except the devotion we choose to offer. Surrender is immense. From its heights, the abyss softly calls, reminding us of a depth beyond the restless surface of things. In the darkness, something waits—rich with unseen forms, waiting to be revealed.

6

# The Door Is in the Darkness

## MARINA BORRUSO

> If we look for the Divine outside, there is no exit. The Divine exists in the darkness, in getting into everything that we do not like about ourselves and that we would like to put a patch on so as not to see it. That is where the exit is.
>
> —MARINA BORRUSO

There once was a man who sat on a park bench nearly every day for two years. An odd, ageless man, he spoke to no one. Like a happy child, he had accidentally opened the door that leads out of time. Swimming in joyful water, he played with the boundaries of things. Around him, the wheels of life kept turning. His name was Eckhart Tolle, and he was immersed in an ocean of presence. We know him now as the author of *The Power of Now*, the best-selling book he wrote after his sudden spiritual awakening and for which he became a highly regarded figure in the transmission of the principles of non-dual wisdom in the West.

I am in Turin, a stone's throw from the Po River, to speak with Marina Borruso, a student of Eckhart Tolle's, the Italian translator of his books, and a powerful teacher in her own right. Marina lives the nondual message in an embodied way—its essence vibrates in her form, in her voice, and in the blissful pauses between sentences when she speaks. Her words are precious vectors, all pointing to a single, unwavering point—a point that ripples if you truly listen.

"I was born in Palermo, by the sea," she begins. "As a girl I used to dive into the water, and there was always that blue space of silence." She continues on to tell me about water meditation, a practice that she teaches and leads at her house in Tuscany. It involves meditating underwater and letting all beliefs dissolve in the suspended grace of floating. We soon find ourselves bathed by the morning light. Her hair reminds me of a fluffy sea sponge, and in her dark, intense yet kind gaze, I encounter presence.

***You teach a lot about presence. Where is the Divine in presence?***

"Many times, the clichés of thought slip into practice," Marina responds. "What ideas do we have of the Divine? Is it something to be achieved, something superior? Is it something special? Is it something that I am not? Is there something I do not want to see in myself and so I grasp at an idea of the Divine? Everything is sacred. Absolutely everything. Everything is alive, and we are it.

"There is a very beautiful Indonesian story that I often tell. A man had been locked inside a cave. He had limited time to find the exit. They would lower food down to him from above, through a hole. For a certain number of days, he would have food, and then that was it. He would scramble for the light, to reach the hole from where the food came down. He hoarded everything he could find to reach that spot, but he could not reach it and soon died. When people later entered the cave to retrieve his body, the light they carried illuminated a hole in the floor right next to the man. The hole had been in the darkness, and he had only looked toward the light. The exit out of the situation he was in was into the darkness. It is the same for us. If we look for the Divine outside, there is no exit. The Divine exists in the darkness, in getting into everything that we do not like about ourselves and that we would like to put a patch on so as not to see it. That is where the exit is.

"Surely it has happened to you that when there is an inner resistance, and you finally take care of it, then a space opens that you can also physically feel: an expansion, a lightness. The inner waters finally move because that heaviness was like a log that prevented the river from flowing. I liken this journey toward presence, and toward the Divine being that we are, to a giant slalom. The slalom gates are what we do not like about us. They are the darkness. If you do not pass through them, if you do not enter them, then you are always projecting into the future, and such a race never begins or ends because it remains an illusion of your mind. Instead, as great teachers have said for millennia, it is all alright. It is all here. We are already what we want to become. But until you have the experience, it is hard to know this."

It seems that our ego is made up of these slalom gates—parts we refuse to see, resistances. If the ego is somewhat like a fortress, then we must absolutely desire to open its gates. It barricades itself to create a sense of protection, though in truth, none is needed. So, one may choose to confront these knots. On the spiritual journey, inevitably, one will have to pass through these gates and these resistances.

***Are unresolved knots in our ego-personality getting in the way of accessing the witness state or blocking our inner journey at some point?***

"Of course they are," Marina affirms. "In fact, these blocking nodes are the door. We just do not recognize them as such. We say, 'For goodness' sake, not this!' But though this is not what you want, it is what it is. That is why surrendering to what is present is so important. This is not the kind of surrender we usually talk about but a surrender that comes from present attention, intelligent attention. This distinction is very important.

"Mental attention wants a result; it is the mind of the past and the future, which knows no present. The temporal mind is constantly jumping from the past to the future, bypassing the present. For example, when we listen to music while being situated in our temporal mind, we realize this as a judgment arises like *I like it* or *I don't like it*, or we recognize and name, *Ah, that's the clarinet, that's the piano*. What does this mean? That at that moment, we are not in the present, we have gone backward, we have gone through the files of the past and judged. We do this constantly.

"Here, we are not interested in the attention-that-wants-something but in the present attention that includes the body. Present attention follows the breath, feels the feet or the bottom of the chair or any part of the body. It's a kind of attention that includes the body and looks at what is there without wanting anything. It has no future to reach. It surrenders, because it allows. Surrender is not something you do; surrender happens when you shift to another attention that is already at peace. It welcomes, it listens, it realizes what is there, and it lets it be. That is, surrender is basically the wisdom of recognizing what is present, and while what is present may not be so good, it is what it is.

"Mental attention is the ego; it is the idea of who I am. The ego is an idea, an idea that goes with all the corresponding emotions. So of course it blocks because it makes one lean toward things. To think, *I want to enlighten myself* is nonsense! When we think *I want to enlighten myself*, we think that it implies that we will have this, that, and the other. I have known some enlightened ones up close; they have none of that. They get angry; they have difficulties in life. There is a whole fantasy around us becoming enlightened and going to heaven. There is nothing like that. We are already what we are, humbly, with what is there. And if we do not like it, well, that is what there is.

"Eckhart tells the story of Epictetus, the Greek slave who surrendered so much to his situation that the Roman who owned him realized that there was no point in keeping someone who was so free. Epictetus was freed and went back to Greece, opened a school, and started teaching."

Freedom. Imprisonment. While on a retreat a short while before my conversation with Marina, it became very clear to me that, inwardly, I am in a prison—a very advanced, sublime, and sophisticated complex of habits of thought, energetic tendencies, and ways of doing and not doing. No matter how much I struggled to find a way out, I couldn't. My shackles felt like something physical, as if I were made of this very restriction. One of those days, as I was meditating, a voice managed to penetrate these walls and said, *Relax, you are in prison.* It was a very open and joyful voice, a free voice, so it was easy to hear. *Right,* I thought to myself. *What is the point of struggling? If I am stuck in here, I might as well relax.* A deep relaxation then spread through my whole being. I started laughing and felt the fiery heat of that deep laughter in my belly and my arms. My face exploded into a thousand sparks. As I melted, it was as if I changed states and became something liquid or gaseous—something to which bars and walls are irrelevant.

This small awakening didn't solve everything. The prison is still there like a rusty old trap, and whether I feel locked in it or not depends on the state I am in. The more solid I am—that is, the more identified with the idea of myself (the ego) and the temporal mind—the more the impression of being stuck and limited arises. The more I allow space within, the more I am in tune with the flow of life, with present attention, the less "trapped" I feel. In that state, being is in no way limitable.

***I recently had an experience of freedom from my ideas and the self-imposed prison I was in. Is accepting what is the best way to free oneself from any hold?***

"Acceptance is not something I do, and it is not something I do when there is something I do not like," Marina cautions. "That creates an addiction to having things I do not like so that I can practice. Many people write to me saying, 'Ah, I'm lucky to have so many difficulties—it means I have lots of opportunities to surrender.' Surrender is a state, and one can surrender even to good things, even to things one loves, to enthusiasm, to joy. Surrender is an inner state, but it can only come from the present; otherwise, what do you surrender to?

"The body is the key. Everything happens and reverberates in the body. The body holds—in the cells, in the tendons, in the bones, in the organs—all the memories of what we have experienced, and what we have inherited from our parents, from the place and time in which we were born. Because all the memories are in the body, the body is the setting in which we can do this cleansing. In the body, we can encounter everything that it is important to get in touch with and let go of. We can feel all the logs that block the flow of awareness through sensations, emotions, and our organs.

"You have probably had the experience of walking into a house and immediately wanting to leave. Or you meet a person, and you immediately feel *Mmm, no*, while with other people you feel *Mmm, yes*. Just as a house holds the memory of what has been experienced, just as the earth holds the memory of everything that has happened, the body also has a memory of everything we have experienced.

"I work a lot with spontaneous body movement. By letting the body do whatever it wants, parts that we generally do not move or that we move with structured exercises (which therefore maintains structure) start to move. We need to destructure. Spontaneous movement uses the body's intelligence to let it do what it wants, how it wants. Then extraordinary things happen—the body comes alive.

"There is a story from the time of the Sun King in France. A Catholic priest had gathered a group of people to shake their bodies in a garden in front of the church. Miraculous healings happened. The king began to worry and sent soldiers to disrupt the gathering.

But those who were shaking were invincible; there was no stopping them. As a result, the church was closed, and a famous sage posted a humorous sign: 'By order of the Sun King, God can no longer make miracles in this place.'"

In telling this story, Marina "shook" in front of me in her chair, making the audacity of what this group did even more vivid and making this perhaps my favorite teaching story of all time. It is a beautiful image: a group of bodies shaking in front of a church, radically questioning the tyranny of the rigid body, a millenarian regime.

"Let all that you are manifest with spontaneity," Marina continues. "The attention that observes is the attention that allows, that uses the natural wisdom of the body to finally move toward the recognition that you are already enlightened, that everything has already happened, that everything is already there.

"Do we let the body move at its will? No. We force it. It is always limited. What happens if you let the body move as it wants to, without trying to understand or to do? Doing is the place of the ego. The ego is confirmed by doing."

At this moment I realize I do not know how to be in the body spontaneously. Right now, the feeling of a fist of energy is forming at the center of my chest, so I ask about it.

"If you feel a stiffness, stay in the feeling," Marina says. "Put your attention there and follow it. If it moves, you also move. Because generally when we put our attention on one thing, it gets bigger. And that's when we run away. But why does the sensation widen? A sensation is a form. It contains, like all forms, vitality. We say 'fear.' In saying 'fear,' we maintain a form because the idea is also a form. So, we put our attention, instead, on the sensation. If you stay in the sensation without naming it, without using the temporal mind, at a certain point you will see that this sensation begins to expand. What is happening? The life, the vitality that is in there, is opening. It is a perfect moment! Let it expand; let it open up. In losing its form, it is giving you all the vital energy that is imprisoned inside.

"That is why we have so little energy and are tired. We have so many of these contracted forms that we have to keep under control. This imprisons vitality. We must cultivate a form of self-control to ensure these tendencies do not emerge at the wrong time, but we must let them be free.

"People worry what will happen if they have a panic attack. This is the natural release of the body that says, 'Enough, I cannot take this load of fear anymore.' All the energy that we have kept underneath explodes. It is beneficial. There is no danger in a panic attack, but the ego sees it as a danger because it cannot control it. The body shows what has not been allowed to express.

"There is an age when children ask you to scare them, as a game. You scare them, and they laugh. First they get scared, and then they laugh. What is that laughter? It is fear opening up. Laughter is the life energy that comes out when fear transforms. We did it as children; we knew how to do it, and we still know how to do it."

***How do we facilitate this change in the energy of the body without doing something? Since the practice is about nondoing, is there an intention that guides us?***

"The intention is the fire," Marina explains. "If you feel that there is something in you that wants to know what this is all about, that impulse is fundamental. Some have it and some do not. You cannot inject it into those who do not, but there are times when life kicks you and that helps you to wake up to the intention.

"Without intention, you do things to satisfy the spiritual ego. There are people who meditate and practice for a lifetime, but nothing changes in them. If the intention is to serve the ego, it does not work; you do not go anywhere. You do not clean anything that is inside, because the ego needs emotions; it needs heaviness. The ego lives on density. These are its investments—'Oh poor me,' 'How shall I do this?' etc."

I confess to her that in listening to one of her talks on the spiritual ego, I cried. Not that I don't cry often anyway, of course. For me, crying seems to be the natural way to release strong emotions. The point is, I realized—although in very good faith—that I have practiced for many years with too much voracity for peace, silence, and stillness, fleeing vast areas of darkness and pain. I felt these areas sometimes, and they occasionally threatened to overwhelm me, but I did not admit it. It is amazing how deluded we can be, how goodwill can slip into the wrong hands, even if those hands are our own. I sense a new ego, more spiritual but no less egoic, has grown in me. This is a cage of fine gold, whereas before I was in a cage of common metal. But the point of the practice is liberation—it is about getting out of the cage, not about painting it or making it shinier.

"Yes, sometimes we miss the point," Marina says. "You have to recognize that you do not know, that you cannot know, that you are in misery, that you are in darkness, and just stay there. That is the practice. That leads you to humility. When spiritual practice is done as ego practice, then you are on your own. You want to achieve something, but that something is not united with totality. There is no experience of totality. Awareness means that you and I are the same thing, we are one. And we are one with this table, with this incense, with this chocolate, with what is there. We are all one.

"How many times does a farmer sit under a tree and have this experience of being one with the tree, one with the grass, one with the stars? It is that. And then you realize that it is not you doing it, but rather things are being done. It is about just saying yes to what is there and embracing your nature, what you are. The mental programming that you have, did you make it? No, you received it. It is there. Some feel the intention, others do not. Is it ill will not to want to know oneself? No. Can anyone be saved from their suffering unless they want to face it? No. The truth is that we do not know; we really do not know anything."

***If we are not standing in the truth of what we are, we do not live authentic lives. How is this revolution of perspective accomplished? How do we learn to observe inward in a way that can lead to liberation?***

"Have you heard of *A Course in Miracles*?" Marina asks. "It is a beautiful support because it allows you to experience many concepts that often become mentally abstract. Let me get it so I can show it to you."

Marina walks into the next room. She returns with an imposing hardcover book covered in blue cloth. This is not a book I am familiar with, and I learn it consists of 365 lessons that were channeled by Helen Schucman in the 1960s. Marina opens it and starts running her finger down the page.

"Lesson 1: Start with what you see," she says. "If you turn your gaze around the room, you will see a chair, a rug, the sofa. You can perhaps perceive that everything you see matches something within you—a memory of what these armchairs, this floor, this table are. *It looks like . . . It reminds me of . . . I wish I had it . . .* In all the first lessons of this book, you work with what you see; hence with your perception. You have a perception of things that you seem to see, but in reality, what are you seeing? The past or the future—in the sense that you will recognize the objects because of the memory of the past and you will project onto some objects desires to be accomplished in the future, such as *I really need to replace the flowers; I'll go buy new ones.*

"By taking this journey, you begin to see that you do not see. You only see what is in your mind! And what is in your mind is conditioned by everything that you feel, have lived, and inherited—by what you wish was not there. When there is an absence of contact with what's real, there is no unity.

"Now, experience this. Look at your hand. Don't move it, just look and see whatever thoughts or judgments come up. Then put your attention on the breath and look at the hand again, but this time continuing to follow the breath. Notice if what you see is the same as before or not. Also notice if there is a sense of unity when you look at it when your attention is on the breath."

I tell her that yes, my hand feels closer.

"Exactly," she says. "That is the experience of the one coming closer. If you start looking at things by including the body and then you look at them from a present attention, the hand, the cupboard, the chair, they become something from which you are no longer separate. Then everything becomes alive. Everything becomes mine in the sense that we are one, not in the sense of the ego.

"I sculpt as a hobby. I had an exhibition and invited those who came to touch, not just look at, the statues. Some musician friends started to sing and play what arose spontaneously in them when they looked at and touched the statue. They began by seeing life in that stone, and simply because their attention shifted, they began to feel. That is also the Divine. It is seeing the Divine in everything, which is not the same as 'the Divine that I must get because I don't like the idea of who I am.'"

I chuckle because, for a long time, I saw the Divine as something I had to reach or attain to "save" me from myself.

***You have a sculpture called* Feminine and Masculine, *which is very beautiful: a single head with a female face on one side and a male face on the other. Could you talk about this polarity that is in each of us? Does it need to be balanced, and if so, how?***

"This is an important question," Marina says. "We are masculine and feminine; we have them both within us. The ego is male, and so our culture supports the dominance of the masculine in women and in men. That is the imbalance. Living in the present and removing the obstacles of suffering within us harmonize the two. We see clearly, in our culture, the loss of inner harmony between the masculine and the feminine. It is not a question of preferring one over the other but of removing the obstacles so that nature can return to its balance.

"When we do this, we realize that everything we do cooperates, from what we eat to the movements we make—everything. How much conscious attention do we put into what we eat? How do we eat? How do we sleep? When we are sleepy, do we sleep? No. When we are hungry, do we eat? No. It starts from there. Everything leads to awareness; everything leads to the so-called awakening. Everything leads to embracing our nature. The body suggests what we want to eat, but do we listen to it? No. I have done many seminars on food. Seminars where you eat! And a lot of historical and archaeological deposits of emotions come up for people. Many people have disorders like bulimia and anorexia that are deposits of unheard things. Food takes us back to the beginning of life, to acceptance, to union with another being.

"Every aspect of life matters and is related to practice. Another example is money. How do you use it? What do you do with it? What do you think of it? What do you do to get it? Money is an energy, which implies a responsibility. Do you use it for your well-being or for your discomfort? Do you use it for the well-being of the world? How do you use it? What do you do with this energy that arrives? It all leads to recognizing and harmonizing our true nature."

***As we set the process of awareness in motion and awaken our sensitivity, it sounds like you are saying emotional content that has been compressed since the dawn of our lives (and perhaps even from before) can emerge. How can we take care of ourselves and become mothers to ourselves, caring for pains whose origin we do not even know? How can we embrace our whole being in a radical way?***

"Sometimes at the end of a retreat people ask me, 'How can I return to the world with all this sensitivity?'" Marina tells me. "Sensitivity awakens. There are compulsive behaviors that we have accumulated. This is a fundamental point—that when we come into this life, when we incarnate, we have a Buddha mind, an original and clear mind. That original mind is wise; it knows. Children know. Up to a certain age, children know and understand because they have that original mind. The original mind recognizes a singing bird, the wind blowing, and the sound of the water. It needs no explanation. It is a mind that knows. We think that we have lost that original mind, but this is not true. We still have it; it is always there. It is our wise part, the part of us that saves us in those moments when it seems that all is lost.

"But what happens to children as they encounter matter? They encounter the density, the suffering, the disappointment that matter brings. So, even if the people around them love and care for them—which is usually the case because otherwise none of us would have survived—the contact with that disappointment is very strong; the child cannot remain in contact with that disappointment, and so they detach. In detaching, little by little, they lose contact with the original mind, with their true nature, and begin to believe that the disappointment will accompany them through life. All compulsive behaviors come from this.

"When the intention is awakened, then the original mind, the Buddha mind, the knowing mind, the wise mind also begins to awaken. And it no longer believes in delusion. As it no longer believes in delusion, it does not get attached to the compulsive behaviors that are the ones that lead to delusion. It is not complicated. It does not need theories. The truth is essential; it is simple. We all have access to the truth. We recognize it inwardly."

Marina invites me to visit her in Tuscany when I return from my trip to India. But only two months after my conversation with her, she left her body. Teachers, masters, never die; they simply move into the largest room there is, and they are always available to us. They teach in life, and they teach forever. I am profoundly grateful to have had the opportunity to meet her at least once, to dive with her into the present, to witness her beauty.

When something arises within me that I don't want to face—which is quite often actually—and I turn away, I remember Marina saying, "The door is in the darkness!" We must nurture the most unruly and restless aspects of ourselves, let them be, and allow the messes to dissolve into the sky of awareness. Whenever we want to cover something up, we should instead sit with that discomfort, fully inhabit it, and breathe into it. This is how we become mothers to ourselves, and this is the way into the Divine, always available to us, no matter what happens outside.

I am grateful to Marina for this important lesson: The Divine is neither distant nor remote. It is not secluded in a "higher" dimension accessible only through special practices. The Divine is within reach—if we choose to reach for it. And to access it, the door is not necessarily one of light leading to the familiar radiance of a paradise we have been taught to expect and manifest. A spirituality willing to venture into the dark becomes profoundly real and near because each of us carries our own darkness. When we step into the dark unknown and set free what is in the unconscious, we draw it into the light with gentle strength, compassion, and love. We don't dispel the darkness; we allow it to unfold within the light.

A darkness in which you can walk and see is no longer frightening. A darkness in which you can breathe peacefully is no longer suffocating. This isn't about embarking on a mission "in search of our dark spots." They emerge spontaneously, constantly. They are found in the microfrictions of daily life, the recurring conflicts with certain triggering events or people, and the countless nuanced encounters with our shadows, which are far from simply gray. Our inner river of life is often scattered with numerous logs jamming up the flow. These logs are our constant resistances—to love, to gratitude, to serenity. Within us lies an ancient, deeply ingrained habit, solid as stone: the habit of resisting the present and its immense gift. Human life is mostly about contraction and habit, which is resisting life itself. The darkness within us is all the life we refuse to meet, yet it knocks at our door, relentlessly.

Why has it been stowed away? Probably because seeing it is painful. But it is no coincidence that most people come to spirituality through the doorway of pain. It is there that life is truly seen, and its wholeness fills us. We are consciousness capable of freeing consciousness, and sometimes the void we try to fill is a void of vision—we fail to see life in its full depth, and so we miss being nourished by such fullness, which is not rational, is not logical—it is Divine.

When we pay closer attention—an attention softened by kindness and compassion—we find within the body a safe harbor from which to gaze at the ocean. And suddenly, life can become a continuous field of discovery and a welcoming place. Darkness does not protect us from pain. Anchored in bodily awareness, guided by the breath that knows how to soothe us, we can make ourselves available to see.

As women, or men, who feel called to embrace this approach, we can learn to relate to the darkness with creativity. There are times when we don't fully understand what's happening within us; we succumb to negativity, withdraw, act impulsively, or cling to greed. In those moments, we are touching the darkness. If we can bring awareness to these experiences, we might find release—through tears, anger, or some other transformation of energy. Something long buried within us may finally be set free when we meet it with caring attention.

We don't always know where these feelings come from or why they arise when they do. Yet this inner darkness holds the potential to bring us closer to our whole selves. By listening to what emerges, we can respond with compassion. Perhaps we'll sense the need to take a long walk in the woods, light candles and soak in a warm bath, or set firmer boundaries with others. Whatever the response, we don't have to fear our own darkness. Instead, we can sit with it, knowing that what we meet there can deepen our understanding of ourselves and life.

It is as though someone is knocking at the door of our heart. These are the guests we've kept hidden in the shadows. Now is the time to welcome them and discover how vast and spacious our inner world truly is.

7

# Dancing with Darkness and Light

## PARAMJYOTI CAROLA STIEBER

Whoever listens carefully to what their body wisdom says and to what story their movements are telling—even if they're being moved by strong emotions—can experience transformation and healing.

—PARAMJYOTI CAROLA STIEBER

Paramjyoti crosses my path in Assisi, the holy place of Saint Francis and Saint Clare in Italy. She wears a burgundy dress crafted perfectly for one who seeks to wear only what is essential and indispensable. There is something transcendent about her, and the word *soul* floats through my mind. Her long, bell-cut dress is ideal for a swirling dance, but her otherwise sober style reflects an inner elegance that allows the essential to be more visible to those willing to see it.

From a young age, Paramjyoti was drawn to dance, as a spiritual and artistic practice. She is the founder of Devadasi—Dance of the Heart school. *Devadasi* means "female servant of God," and even today in South India, devadasis marry a deity and devote themselves to a life of ritual—a life that revolves around dancing for the Divine.

We meet at the Ananda community, a spiritual center inspired by Paramahansa Yogananda's teachings that provides training in meditation, yoga, and a cooperative way of living based on divine consciousness and inner joy. As she wants to be outdoors, we leave the veranda to sit in the woods behind the temple. We sit opposite each other on a wooden tent platform where summer retreatants stay. The forest is thick with slender trees; there is a strong smell of resin and the impression of sitting in a shadow. The sky above us is mostly overcast, which makes the forest feel protective, as if it were a roof over our heads.

When a friend from the Ananda community told me they had a woman visiting who dances for the Divine, I knew I had to speak with her. Among all the ways to marry the Divine as a woman, I hadn't considered the path of dance as prayer. As a child, I spent many years in rhythmic gymnastics and classical ballet, and I hold memories of those moments when, dancing before a vast audience, a divine sensation would arise—life was entirely there; nothing else existed in that moment. In surrendering my body to the present, I truly encountered something greater. But spirituality later became something else for me—a rigorous effort to sit in silence with chaos, aiming straight for my heart while trying not to force anything. At this stage, I welcome an expanded notion of the Divine and am curious to hear about dance as a sacred path.

***What does it mean to dance for the Divine? What is a sacred dance?***

"I like to ask this question of my students," Paramjyoti answers. "What does it mean to dance not for the sake of name or fame or for political statements or artistic expressions or for selfish purpose or personal reasons or in the name of whatever conflict inhabits and occupies the artist's mind? I had an injury in my second year at the dance academy, and I was compelled to search deeper into my personal motivation for dancing. As a dancer, you are taught to become anything. You are an instrument. You empty yourself and make yourself available. I want to dance what is true in the moment, in a fresh way, as I am talking to you now. Movement is my way of combining soul, heart, and body—of communicating holistically from that perspective, from the present moment. This is the key I have been given: to align whatever arises in the mind with breath and movement. It is very simple. And if there is nothing in my mind, all the better!"

In many spiritual traditions, the body is considered secondary. We are called to experience who we truly are, and invariably, it is said that we are not the body. This is undoubtedly true. We identify with the body, yet it is merely a vessel for our consciousness, which evolves through human experience in the material world. For women, in particular, the body holds great significance. If we choose to become mothers, it becomes the place of gestation. It is where pleasure arises, where we feel our strength—our physical strength. It is a space of expression. We love to adorn ourselves, to be creative with our bodies. Thus, this sacred path in which the body itself becomes a prayer strikes me as profoundly feminine. From the way Paramjyoti talks about dance, I can see that she has a very deep attunement with the breath. I ask her to tell me more about the trio of breath-body-mind and their interactions.

"During the dance," she says, "you put your attention on the breath and on everything you feel as an observer. If there is mental or emotional content, there is something to dance with. For example, if people have an inner conflict, then there is something very concrete to dance with.

"Once, while dancing a ninety-minute improvised performance, at one point I felt like I was cheating. I had danced for about thirty minutes, but suddenly there was no longer a truly alive inspiration to keep moving. I had nothing more to say. I asked myself whether

I should simply continue dancing something that had no true importance to me or stop. There was a conflict, for people had paid for their ticket to watch the dance. How could I suddenly just simply stop the performance? In that moment, the inspiration came to me that I could draw information from the individuals in the audience. I started to dance for someone. This created immediate engagement. The game changed. There was no longer a performer and a passive audience. Everyone sat on the hot seat thinking that they might be the next ones I would dance for and wondering what would happen if I did!

"Dancing for individuals in the audience completely changes the chemistry in the room. First, there is a real and living encounter, and then it seems that divine inspiration participates because my body takes forms and tells stories that I cannot possibly know because these are strangers. When this Shakti, or grace, manifests, it is very moving—both for the audience and for the dancer—for it is like being in the service of a very high inspiration, a deep knowingness. As this force manifests, we can witness it. It becomes tangible to our physical ears and eyes."

This is new to me; I have never heard of such an approach: the audience as the raw material for the performance. They come to witness a beautiful dance, but they may instead receive a dance that speaks about them directly to them—a dance that eventually unveils aspects and facets that they were not aware of or feel very moved and touched by. They experience being seen, and they witness some unexplainable knowingness. The tangled skein of yarn they carry within unravels before their eyes, revealing something long buried, knotted, or concealed.

I imagine Paramjyoti dancing for me. What would the threads of my numerous entanglements look like? I dare not ask her. I try to put myself in her shoes. It must be very peculiar to lay yourself so bare in receptivity, to be like a screen on which the inner life of another is imprinted.

"This magic is to me like a real kiss of the Divine," Paramjyoti reveals. "When I dance for someone, it is something unique. Each time, I feel like I have never danced something like it before. The ingredients that make up that moment—the feeling, the energy, the intention, the attention, the state of consciousness—make it fresh. It is not something that comes from memory."

***How would you describe this form of improvisation? What do you need to do to move in such a way?***

"It is emptying oneself and putting oneself at the service of something more, making oneself available to what wants to be seen and reflected," Paramjyoti explains. "Sometimes, there is a story that I later can tell. Sometimes, there is no need for me to know, and the mind remains empty. At other times, the people I dance for tell me what they discovered or what they saw in the reflection of their own energy. It is a channeling that allows you to return home through your personal matrix, or inner construct. You do not need the matrix of Mary, Jesus, or Yogananda. Obviously, it is beautiful and touching to connect to these forces, but to become true and return home, you might as well go directly. The flower that comes from you or her or him is unique and has its own expression. I nurture everyone's unique flower."

Always curious about how to shift ourselves into this receptive state, I wonder if this is something available to all of us.

***What must be there for the dance to be activated?***

"A 'you' has to be there," Paramjyoti says. "Here is a little philosophy: When we say, 'God and I,' we create a duality, but are they two elements or one? Does one appear in the other? Is it *dvaita* or *advaita*, duality or nonduality? There are saints who foster in their hearts both perspectives simultaneously. Dance is a dialogue. It comes to life between these polarities.

"For me, dance must have a meaning. It needs to make sense, be it a dance for the Divine Mother, or a dance for an audience. If someone, for example, requests a dance, and I can be of service, then dancing makes sense to me."

***In what way does dance become sacred, like a prayer? What is the alchemy of the heart that allows the body to become an instrument of the Divine?***

"As a teacher, I feel I do not have to serve a ready-made meal to my students," Paramjyoti answers. "I invite everyone to prepare their own meal and then to find out together what makes the difference—is it more or less salt—and so on. If I provide mental answers about what dance is or what makes it sacred, something falls flat. But let us see if I can at least give you an idea. Motivation is our initial driving force. What makes me move? Is it to please somebody? Is it to satisfy my own pleasure or physical need? Is it for personal expression? What is my inspiration for moving? And why? What for? That sets the tone of the dance—it may become a prayer or something sacred. You identify a meaning and direct the energy and, according to that, you harvest. Inspiration and inner motivation are the basis. And you can dance even by moving just one finger."

I think of Michelangelo's fresco painting the *Creation of Adam*, the famous meeting of the fingers of God and Adam. I have always felt this painting was like a dance. The finger of God, which is more active, reaches out to touch the finger of Adam, which is more passive. The fingers here represent a turn of grace, a secret dance of the heart in the movement of separation and reunion. And one cannot forget Leonardo da Vinci's enchanting painting *Saint John the Baptist*, in which Saint John points his index finger toward the heavens with a smiling gaze. A finger, if moved by the right intention, can move mountains.

"Another miracle happens when the vessel for the harvest—the dancer—is purely empty and calls for God, who has never gone anywhere, of course," Paramjyoti continues. "At that moment, the spirit can be experienced. When I dance for someone, I can feel that there is something in the air. I like the German term *herz-geist*, heart-mind. The word itself, in my personal interpretation, describes this holy union. You cannot separate the mind and heart; they belong together, and together they come into action.

"I work with many approaches to cultivate this connection between heart-mind, including meditation, visualization, and invocation. I often use the image of a radio. Just like with a radio, we can tune our awareness to different channels. Radio blah blah, for example, is the monkey mind. It is the constant chitchatting. But there are other channels we can tune in to. I cannot say that there is one specific way to tune our radio to the frequency of the herz-geist, for the path is very individual. Everyone must find the ingredients that make alchemy possible in their own hearts."

Since Paramjyoti previously mentioned that the essential ingredient of dance is the presence of a "you," I wonder whether emotions themselves—often arising as powerful forces within us—are not only something that naturally emerges during dance but also something one can dance with.

***How do you dance with emotions?***

"Emotions move us," replies Paramjyoti. "They play an important role. In some forms of meditation, we are invited to let the emotions go—to not hold on to them or pay too much attention to them. I take a more tantric or immediate approach: I want to integrate, face, and eventually move through these emotions. Of course, they are still part of radio blah blah. They are a manifestation of what are called the *vrittis* in the yogic tradition, the 'waves' of disturbance that arise upon a calm sea of mind. In dance, emotions become your partner, and practices like the Tibetan Buddhist *tonglen* can facilitate that dance. In tonglen, whatever we perceive and feel is breathed into the heart, where it is allowed to dissolve. In breathing out, we send compassion to the individual or to the world. Tonglen is a way of working with emotions. For example, you can choose to dance with aspects of yourself that scare you. Usually what happens is that it becomes quite fun! Every shadow holds a gift, offering lessons as we integrate the aspects we often seek to reject.

"In dance, the body does not lie. The body and its movements are truthful and innocent. For the dancer, the body has words. It is expressing beauty, and lies disturb the heart. Movements are the words with which the dancer writes poetry. Whoever listens carefully to what their body wisdom says and to what story their movements are telling—even if they're being moved by strong emotions—can experience transformation and healing."

Every shadow has its opposite side, which is revealed when we invite it to dance. I take a little pause to internalize this image, knowing that the reminder will be useful in those times when my shadow-escape program is triggered. Just as Marina Borruso suggested that we allow shadows to dissolve in the light of presence, we can invite them to dance and create the same effect. It is about letting them emerge while remaining the observer—being the audience of oneself. Dancing with them as they emerge, letting them rise to the surface of the body and allowing them to move the body, expressing what could not otherwise be heard or embraced, adds a note of deep intimacy and radical acceptance. Replacing blind reactions—or hours of still meditation on the cushion—with lyrical, fluid responses sounds like a refreshing and elegant way to transform the mind.

"I once experienced a strong conflict within me," Paramjyoti goes on to share. "No matter what I ate, I still felt hungry. It was like having wolves in my belly. They always wanted more, and nothing could satisfy them. I said to myself: *OK, I can dance with the wolves*. In that instant, the power dance was born. I asked one of my students, who has the mighty physical stature of a bear, to drum for me and hold the space. I asked him to do nothing else besides drum until my dance was finished. We lowered the blinds so that there would be darkness. I turned on the altar light and howled and danced. A miracle happened of the kind that does not happen always but can happen often: With one dance, my internal conflict dissipated.

"Once you meet what you must meet, then you become free from it. The unresolved issue is seen and recognized. You no longer need it. A space opens up in which you can give birth to and unmask the illusion instead of mentally telling yourself that your fear is an illusion and avoiding facing it. An important aspect in a power dance is the presence of someone to hold the space—a witness who maintains a neutral, nonjudgmental presence. There are other subtler ways to move through one's emotions too; it is not always necessary to go into the catharsis, into the unfathomable depths of your valleys, but I think it is very nice that this possibility exists."

I am fascinated by the idea of dancing with one's shadows—of encountering the wolves that are howling in one's guts, the insatiable hunger itself, and whatever other demons need nourishment. There is something pacifying and ancestral about the image of a body dancing with something as invisible and tender as one's own unrecognized and habitually rejected interiority.

I am reminded of the many ways to approach this work: There are those who like to confront head-on and those who use less direct but still effective ways to deal with the hostile forces that we encounter on our path. If one does not have enough awareness, one can get lost. The "demon" can sweep away the inner witness and annihilate it, so the witness, someone to hold the space, is critical. By dancing with darkness, we invite ourselves to acknowledge it while simultaneously letting it go; we allow ourselves to see it and give it its place, while also remaining anchored in ourselves. From this perspective, it seems that darkness teaches us not so much about light but more about the thin line that exists between bringing it out and keeping it in, between admitting it and denying it. It teaches us to find our place within ourselves and to keep ourselves situated there—to make a home within ourselves and keep the flame lit. In this way, dance "localizes" awareness.

"I like to give space to what arises while keeping presence active, like a raised antenna," continues Paramjyoti. "This does not mean that I lean toward the light. Presence is more of a neutral point, a zero point, where brightness and shadow cancel each other out. Perhaps I can say that the heart of being has its own (neutralizing) intelligence and that our attention can be brought back to this place.

"The most interesting thing—and the most spiritual one—is to witness that wherever the birth of a manifestation takes place, there also exists the unmanifest. I am interested in dwelling in that space that allows for all kinds of dances and all kinds of encounters. From this perspective, the play of manifestation—with its infinite faces, lights, and shadows—as well as the recognition of the nonmanifest, is present."

It occurs to me that the space that exists before a manifestation—the "witnessing consciousness"—is not a physical space, nor does it exist in a linear, time-bound way. The word *before* might suggest that the witness comes first, preceding the event, but in truth, the witness exists outside of time altogether. It is a presence that holds space for what arises, a neutral awareness that allows both light and shadow to emerge without being swept away by them. Because our language lacks precise terms for this, we use these words as approximations, understanding that they are not meant to be taken literally.

As my conversation with Paramjyoti continues, I realize I am not the one leading this dance, that it is she who is guiding me onto the dance floor, where I can slowly shed my ideas and concepts.

"The first approach in the dance of the heart is to move with your attention and awareness toward the source of inspiration," she says. "In classical ballet or modern dance, we strive to become the perfect form. This too empties the vessel. There is no time to think because we receive hundreds of commands to realize the form: stomach in, ribs in, open your chest, chin up, shoulders down, legs outstretched, do not get stiff, breathe, and so on. As mantras, these commands give the monkey mind something to hold on to so that it can become empty. This I would call a 'positive' dance—one where we empty ourselves to reproduce a perfect form. In a 'negative' dance, on the other hand, we go inward, listen to the breath, and receive the images. We breathe into the heart. The form comes from within, from feeling. We feel what is there to be danced from this interior place. It is not an external, already decoded image. It is a free movement that emerges when we move toward the source."

***How do you teach people who have never danced before to bring into form externally what they perceive internally?***

"It is not easy," Paramjyoti admits. "How do you translate anger or joy into movement? Step-by-step. It is like making a braid. Several strands come together: the dance technique, the ability to be aware of the physical body and of the subtler bodies, and improvisation. How can we let the body speak and say what is inside through a vocabulary of movements? There is also the spiritual practice, with its meditation and visualizations—all these things must come together.

"Depending on who I have in front of me, I typically understand where to start, which tools to give first and which come later. Everyone has their own map. Groups, too, have their own dynamic. I work with the same basic principles, emphasizing different aspects depending on what's needed. But you cannot truly separate these things; you cannot separate working on the body from working on the spirit."

Often, when we express ourselves—especially as women—we face criticism coming from within that has been shaped by voices we've internalized from others, like a judgmental parent or authority figure. These sabotaging, critical voices can hold us back, preventing us not only from expressing ourselves but also from truly knowing and embracing who we are. I ask Paramjyoti about how to meet the judgment that arises while dancing.

"Of course, judgment arises from the ego, which we cannot get rid of," she says. "The dancer has to be ready for the miracle of being empty, or the next step. I am only the midwife. In my journey, personally, there has been a lot of liberation. It is a constant endeavor to move within the unknown. This is what makes the process so rich. The known has its limits—a beginning and an end—but to dare to take a step into the unknown is deadly scary. Everything comes fully alive! The adrenaline comes, and the inner quest for what is truly important comes alive again. Every technique and every method of dance serves this inner journey, so we can eventually experience pure consciousness, pure awareness. The question becomes, How do we access it? How do we stay there? How do we rest in that which we already are?"

There is an exquisite charge in the air, and I experience that optical effect that occurs after staring into someone's eyes uninterrupted for some time—the forest background becomes a green blur, and Paramjyoti's face seems painted like a watercolor. Her gaze is vivid and direct. She offers her whole self, and I become absorbed by it, creating a subtle tension in my body, which immediately relaxes as I notice it. I hear the birds humming, and suddenly everything seems like a dance in my heart. I exhale deeply.

***How does dance embody the pure Shakti, the feminine principle—the energy of movement, of form, of becoming?***

"The body is the first expression of Shakti; it is the form," Paramjyoti asserts. "But we also dance with the spirit, which we can call Shiva, if you like. Dance is Shakti as well as Shiva. How can there be Shakti without Shiva? Dance might be a rather feminine expression of their duo, yes, but it includes both. Dance is the most immediate form of a call to the present moment. It leaves no trace. It is in no way separate from Shiva, from the male principle, from the witness. I believe it is an eternal dance between these two principles. It is the simultaneous existence of space and its absence, of time and its absence. It is constant change, constant renewal. I cannot say it is more Shakti than Shiva. If there were no Shiva, no awareness of Shakti, how could we even speak of Shakti? When I dance, I feel the soul, rather than the masculine or the feminine. Of course, sometimes one or the other force prevails, but I tend to dance from a neutral position."

***What about the dance between music and silence?***

"For me," Paramjyoti says, "the music I dance to has to be played live. I do not work with recorded music because only when music is played live is it possible for music and dance to come from the same inspiration and to emerge together in the here and now. Recorded music obviously belongs to the past and, in listening to it, you are forced into something that is not emerging in the here and now. When both the dancer and the musician are devoid of any concept about what is going to be played or danced, we may discover unity, the mystery of timelessness, or other mystical experiences.

"At a certain point, music and silence become one. Only when I am in duality, out of the mystical union, do I realize that maybe the music does not sound the way I want it to, or I have some other judgment. In the moment of mystical union, is there music or silence? Once you get past the wave of *I like it* or *I do not like it*, you enter that dimension where silence and music are the same thing. At that point, movement and absence of movement are the same thing.

"I work a lot in silence with my students to establish the connection with the self—with the music of one's heart or the silence of inner presence. Once you have established a dialogue with yourself, you can introduce a third element, which can be the musician or the audience. Having established your inner relationship with yourself, you will not easily be enraptured by the music or the perceptions received from your environment. The first and most important point for the practitioner, therefore, is to establish the internal dialogue. The holy spirit cannot fail to come once that dialogue is alive."

A few drops of rain begin to fall on the wooden platform we are sitting on—nature's dance free-falling from above.

***Is it possible to dance for the Divine Mother?***

"Of course," Paramjyoti replies. "Having danced in different spiritual contexts, for Christians, Sufis, Hindus—in Krishna temples as well as Shiva—I can say that the Shakti of the Divine Mother is different from the energy of other aspects of the Divine. It is true that there is a divine principle, but it has so many different colors! It is the same across these contexts but also not the same. You can experience becoming the Divine Mother. I believe that when that *darshan*—the vision or glimpse of a deity, saint, or divine presence—arises, it usually arises as a divine vision that begins to take shape. It does not necessarily arise as a channeling. It is just that that energy takes a form, and the consciousness immerses itself in that energy.

"I would like to add that our imagination is often very alive and that there can be a danger in imagination. People can fall into fantasies. I would not encourage anyone by saying, 'Try to become the Divine Mother.' It is better to simply dance."

In the past few minutes, the rain has become more insistent. We run for shelter and get drenched on the way. Once inside the temple, there is a feeling of unreality, as if we are inside a dream. From the threshold, we look outside, in silence. It's hailing now. The hail is so big that I pick up a piece almost an inch in diameter. Amused, Paramjyoti says, "Look!" In the meadow, the hail is jumping, bouncing, and flying in an endless, merry dance.

For a few minutes, before saying goodbye, there is just that: the dance of the hail in the meadow in the middle of a summer storm and us watching in silence and amazement.

Sometimes, the worst demons are like destructive hailstorms, and we resist dancing with them. Armed with an umbrella, we may discover that those demons are merely stories we haven't read to the end. And, as we allow them to unfold, to take shape in the body, to speak through our movements, we might let it rain until the rainbow comes. Especially for women, this opens an invitation to see the body in a new light: It holds the potential to guide us toward resolving our inner knots. If we can do this in stillness, through meditation, that's wonderful. If not, we can let the body help us. It is an incredible ally on the path of awakening, helping us navigate unpredictable emotional cycles. We already know this from the advice to take a brisk walk to release anger or to engage in a tender yin yoga practice when we feel a need to be held. The body can serve our intention when it aligns with the highest spirit.

When we allow Shakti—the divine, cosmic energy that fuels all creation, transformation, and existence that in Hindu philosophy embodies the dynamic, feminine force of the universe—while staying present, what happens is a divine kiss. We meet that beloved, unseen presence. Pain resolves into wonder, and we are back home. Home is an inner and intimate feeling of knowing. It is a space where we can be completely ourselves. Just as we know our home inside and out, so too can we know ourselves—by reading our stories to the very end, by leaving the doors open. This is how the process of integrating inner understanding with our outer, manifested reality comes to life—by dancing in the house of the spirit.

There is a sense of belonging that comes before all else, before any house or family. It is a feeling of being at home with our being, a birthright to happiness and full self-expression that exists before any external construct. We belong to the unknown, to this mystery that is so familiar to us—so familiar that it feels like our true home—and there is no need to fight gravity anymore.

8

# Embracing Everything, Including Death

## ELENA BROWER

When I sit for zazen, I'm allowing ideas and habit energies to fall away so I can arrive at each circumstance—and eventually my own death—with freshness, readiness.

—ELENA BROWER

It's a sunny day in Santa Fe, New Mexico, and a brilliant light is coming in through the windows. Author, mom, yogini, meditation teacher, poet, artist, mentor, and educator Elena Brower is indefinable; I see a radiant and timeless being, a fusion of extraordinary talents, taste, and embodied awakening.

***How did your spiritual journey begin? What caused you to look within?***

"I was invited to my first yoga class when I was in college," Elena says, "then again post-university in New York City, where I took classes with my boyfriend's mom and sisters. At the end of those classes, I could recall a certain state of being from my childhood, the reverence I felt while sitting in a synagogue during holidays next to my mom, who'd be emotionally moved during the Shema prayer. There was something about the pacing and the quiet that changed me on a cellular level.

"Being accustomed to ballet classes in New York City, where the body was treated as a vehicle, when I was asked to approach my body with kindness and care in yoga class, I felt real resonance. In those early yoga practices, I found myself addressing my body more supportively. Those classes were the beginning of my personal foray into the realms of the spirit."

***Cultivating body awareness seems to be a crucial bridge to heal the perception of a separation between the spirit and matter. How did body awareness become the heart of your work?***

"My own practices have now come into alignment with my teaching, after two-plus decades of teaching what I'd most needed to learn," Elena explains. "In offering my attention to my personal practice, I feel care and kindness naturally arising, both in yoga practice and in zazen [Zen meditation] for these past several years. Through silent attention, I'm beginning to touch compassion for myself, for the experiences of this body, including the traumas endured, mistakes made, reparations offered, and efforts expended.

"The bridge between the body and the spirit, in my experience, is upright attention, wholeheartedly offered, to any moment. We practice it in yoga asanas, in zazen, in caring for other people, in parenting, in relationships, in friendship, and also in circumstances of solitude, quiet. Those moments accrue, rendering us authentic, capable of integrating the uprightness of the body in practice with the ways in which we comport ourselves in our interactions.

"The best example for me personally is in parenting. From an angry, rushed, initially tense template, evolving my communication with my eighteen-year-old son has required practice to become the parent I've always known I could be: present, strong, serene, caring, trusting, and trustworthy."

***So, this awareness, cultivated in whatever we are doing, accumulates over time, drop after drop, and will be more and more available to us if we practice?***

"Yes," Elena agrees, "it takes time. I'll forever be gathering these moments and becoming who I am. One collection of Zen teachings I've been studying comes from the source teacher of Soto Zen, the lineage in which I practice. His name was Eihei Dogen, and he was a Japanese monk who studied with his primary teacher, Rujing, in China, became the abbot of monasteries, and wrote a collection of instructions for the monastery cook, titled the *Tenzo Kyokun*. In these instructions, he offers three heart-minds, or attitudes he implores the cook to cultivate regarding the daily responsibilities of the kitchen, based on his studies in China that he brought back to Japan.

"Studying this book closely for the past two years, offering its themes in my yoga and meditation classes, these instructions have become the basis for my chaplaincy thesis, which is relevant to your question: Attention accrues, in the smallest moments, to become presence.

"The first of the three attitudes is called magnanimous heart-mind. While *magnanimity* implies openness or generosity, a magnanimous mind practices perceiving everything that presents itself as the element of stability. Could even the most painful, difficult event be the element of stability? When a dear friend passes away far too young, how could that be the element of stability? To this tragic truth I bring the practice of magnanimous heart-mind, and I can now see how her release from the pain in her body is a truly stabilizing force—for her and for us who loved her.

"On the days when my son's going skiing and will be doing many backflips at a high velocity, considering his safety and worrying he might suffer a significant concussion—is this, too, the element of stability? Can I sense the steadying force of love behind my fear here? Can I trust that he knows his boundaries and can make his own choices for his body? This is a magnanimous mind.

"The second of the three heart-minds is nurturing mind, also known as parental mind: seeing everything we touch in our lives as though it's a precious child. Food, spices, utensils, plates, our partner's tough day, or a friend's pain. Nurturing mind treats all the seemingly inconsequential details parentally, with great care. That care yields a fresh way of being with all the matters and moments of our lives, moments of attention that indeed accrue. Everything is worthy of our full presence.

"Parental, or nurturing, mind naturally gives rise to the third heart-mind: joyful mind. Seeing everything in this world, every being with whom we interact, through the lens of kinship, the joyful mind sees all beings as our relations. Can we treat even this book in our hands, this present moment of quiet, with appreciation, attention, and joy? Particularly instructive for me in these early years as a Zen practitioner, this practice of joyful mind is leading me to see and address the world with less frustration and more acceptance.

"Cultivating these heart-minds is an invaluable practice, ultimately leading me in the direction of attentiveness."

***You are training to become a Buddhist chaplain. Can you tell me more about this type of service?***

"I am now in my second year of the chaplaincy training at the Upaya Zen Center," Elena replies. "I was introduced to the idea of becoming a chaplain when I began volunteering in a hospice. The Upaya

Zen Center was founded by Abbot Roshi Joan Halifax, my first Zen teacher, who's spent thousands of hours sitting with the dying, offering presence to the people on death row here in New Mexico, traveling to Nepal to bring medical care to remote mountain villages, and transmitting her teachings to clinicians via her programs. Her practice and social engagement move me to release various forms of self-cherishing, so I can look outside myself and see how I can engage and serve in my community.

"Upon learning of the chaplaincy training, after considering the requirements, the time commitment, the teachers, and the possibilities, instantly I felt an anchor drop in my body, a grounding force, even though it seemed I wouldn't have time. Now I'm spending hours each week in three volunteer settings: in prison teaching yoga and meditation to a group of gentlemen, in the local hospice tending to those in the process of dying, and every few weeks serving in grief groups for children and families who've lost family members to illness, death, or deportation.

"Prior commitments have begun falling away so I can do this work, which represents a significant shift in my income. I'm thankful to be spending these years in service. The teachers in the program are luminaries from all fields of life, and I'm having some of the most profound conversations I've ever had. I'm feeling purposeful, on my path."

***One of the big challenges we face, especially as young women, but really at any age, is discovering what's essential in our lives. What do we want to cultivate? Where do we want to devote our time? We get distracted by things we think we can't do without. How does working with and encountering death help us focus?***

"Have you ever been at the bedside of someone who's consciously dying?" Elena asks. "Learning to prioritize listening and just being a steady, silent grounding force in that setting, whether I'm bringing a tray of food or cleaning or changing the bed, it is a practice now.

"Death is a natural process. The *Anguttara Nikaya Sutta*, a collection of Buddhist scriptures, teaches us that we're all of the nature to grow old, to become ill, to die. We will be separated from everything that we love and everybody we care about at some point. Everything dies, and the fact of impermanence asks us to stay open to this, which takes practice. In opening to impermanence, we become free.

"No matter where I am, cultivating a still mind, especially when I want to do, go, and accomplish, is leading me to see that I can allow matters to unfold without interfering and become more accepting, both inwardly and outwardly.

"Being in the presence of someone welcoming death or close to death, especially in places where medical assistance in death is legal, is a real blessing. Bearing witness to a person preparing for their death offers us courageous, deep teachings. Allowing my body to be released peacefully and with love, if given that chance, will be a gift. When I sit for zazen, I'm allowing ideas and habit energies to fall away so I can arrive at each circumstance—and eventually my own death—with freshness, readiness.

"Embracing the natural process of decaying and dying, allowing things to naturally fall away—objects, ideas, opinions, beliefs—we become able to die in peace. As a chaplain, I hope to be part of normalizing these discussions and, as you put it, helping the folks with whom I work to gently embrace their personal process of letting go."

On a flight back home to Italy, just a few days before my conversation with Elena, I was stunned by the staggering beauty of the veil of snow on the highest peaks in the Alps. In an instant, that gorgeous landscape turned into a nightmare. Gusts of wind struck the plane, which suddenly seemed like a paper toy at the mercy of nature's forces. Children were crying, a mother was trying to give everyone courage while setting aside her own fear, and we were all faced in an instant with the terror of dying.

I was surprised by my reaction. I felt a stab of physical pain seeing my attachment to my life, to my story, to everything that had happened to bring me to that moment, to the sheer volume of desire and activity that had driven me—to the chain of events I call my life. This attachment to life was a physical, painful sensation, rooted in the body, in the chest, where the heart is. As I share this with Elena, she nods in understanding. "How did you handle it?" she asks me. I told her that I prayed to Tara, my favorite buddha. The Green Tara is said to be the fastest, coming right in the moment of need, so I intensely recited her beautiful mantra, OM TARE TUTTARE TURE SWAHA.

***How can working with death or the dying help us with this painful attachment to life?***

"The more I bring death into my consciousness, the less fear I feel," Elena shares. "Even with my kid. I have to consider that he could die any day—he does these daring moves on skis—each time I sit I think, *If today is the day, am I awake? If today is my day, if today is my partner's day, am I awake?*

"It's entirely human to resist the idea of death, especially since, as children, most of us weren't raised to see it as a natural part of life. It's somewhere distant from us, over there. The elders are over there, not commonly in our homes. They're somewhere else, so we don't see them. Instead, we're aiming for achievement and growth, ignoring and denying the natural human process of decay and return to the earth, which makes it hard to process death in general. I hope to be part of shifting this for those with whom I'll have the honor of working."

I think immediately of *Softening Time*, Elena's book of poetry, and "Holding Nothing," her newsletter. Like this conversation, and many others I've had for the Women Awakening Project, softness emerges as an important way to relate to oneself and to life, especially as we're doing delicate inner work.

***This softening, or the softness that is tangible in your work, doesn't come naturally to me, but I can feel it's important. How can we move toward softening ourselves?***

"Considering that most of us were raised to achieve and be strong in our culture," Elena responds, "finding softening difficult is common. Especially as women, we've been taught to cultivate our skills and capacities, work ourselves hard, and get there, whatever it takes. As we grow older and wiser, we realize that we've been misled to think that we must compete, win, accomplish. Life becomes so much sweeter, more connected, more present, when we soften.

"Through my forties and now into my mid-fifties, I'm realizing that my softness is vital, for myself and those with whom I interact. Even when someone shows disrespect or seems to be a source of pain in my life, I practice staying open and available to what else might be true. This practice has beneficially impacted everything—my teaching, my practices, my parenting. Offering respect in the face of disrespect has been a lighthouse teaching for me."

***How has walking a spiritual path of growth and self-awareness informed your way of being a mother and vice versa?***

"I started out with an imprint from my parents, particularly my dad," Elena says. "He was twenty-three when I was born—that's so young! I entered my parenting journey with an impression of his unconditional love and affection, as well as his temper, impatience, and immaturity. I was thirty-six when my son was born—old enough to clearly witness those imprints playing out. I had to study it all—my behaviors, words, and attitudes. I had to go through things, like watching my seven-year-old slam a door on me, to release those habit energies. At that time, I began involving him in his own choices, deeply empowering him—these were choices I didn't have as a kid. I asked him for feedback, I listened to his requests, I held good boundaries, and I didn't waver. I practiced being the parent I'd wanted when I was his age, at each stage.

"He was nine when I got sober from alcohol and marijuana, and when many other secretive behaviors ended. Sober and clean, I could just be his mom, nothing to hide. We could have the conversations we needed to have without me being high, and we swiftly grew closer, more trusting of one another. I can thank sobriety for that, as well as my son, and the friends who supported me and the art I was making at that time.

"During the ensuing decade, I managed to write and record a simple audio course for parents called Perceptive Parenting. It involves realizing that we come to parenting with an unconscious idea of what we think is the right way, but then we come to learn that there is a whole person in front of us with a unique set of needs and we have to ask how we meet that reality. That's where spiritual practice comes in—we're being asked, moment by moment, to meet reality as it is, as hard as it might be, even when sitting still. The invitation is simply to stay open to offer an appropriate response."

Women are often advised to stay quiet, to avoid sharing too much. These warnings are fundamentally tied to visibility and the act of openly discussing everyday experiences. It's as if simply speaking up becomes an act of defiance—one that reclaims space, challenges norms, and ultimately empowers women.

***You share your journey very publicly with your community who find inspiration and guidance in your teachings and in the tools you offer. How do you navigate being an example for people and at the same time remain humble, human, and real about it?***

"I've been a student of several different teachers for the past twenty-five years," Elena answers. "I have shifted my focus at a few key moments, and I'm asked with some frequency how I've done that. The real answer is, I have no idea. I just kept following the energy, pivoting when needed. Deep in my heart, I've always sought a woman to be my teacher, and I've found a handful of female teachers at the Upaya Zen Center who can provide real ballast for my spiritual formation. As I get older, I feel less inclined to share, yet I also know that there are certain aspects of my experience that might be of some service to others. Now I'm trying to be more skillful with discernment. I'm learning how to be a better listener, not so quick to offer answers. Asking more questions feels nurturing and supportive now."

***As a teacher, what's the biggest lesson you've learned from your students?***

"I see myself as a student of everything and everyone," Elena says. "I'm always learning, whether it's in a private mentoring setting, a small group mentoring online, or teaching yoga. Returning to a mind of curiosity, I prioritize not knowing, listening well, and not having answers."

This openness—where giving and receiving intertwine—brings me back to the theme of feminine creative power: the ability to create freely, without the need to cling to what has been brought into existence, creating for the sake of creation, offering life what already belongs to it. When this creative power is released from the desire to possess its own creations, it transforms into a profound act of contemplation and meditation. I believe that, as women, we can embrace creativity with far more courage and freedom than we are accustomed to. And once again, this helps us move beyond judgment and inner criticism—especially when we offer our talents in service of something greater than ourselves.

***As a poet, artist, and author, do you find it's possible to direct the creative forces toward finding the beauty and the sacredness of life? Can art be in service of spiritual life?***

"Most of my recent paintings emerge from practice, inspired by artist ancestors who listened intently and then painted what they received, such as Hilma af Klint, Emma Kunz, Agnes Pelton, Agnes Martin, Emily Mason, and Helen Frankenthaler," Elena explains. "The more I practice, the more I'm moved toward writing or painting, and my work keeps evolving with more meaning for me.

"Art is definitely in service to spirit and feels like a direct expression of my practice. Zazen is practiced with eyes slightly open, and some days I emerge from practice with fields of color or washes on my mind that must be painted or they'll be forgotten. I don't know how or why that happens, but I respect it and try to make notes or paint in those moments if I can."

Elena motions toward a simple and beautiful two-color painting behind her.

"There are many layers in these pieces," she continues. "Ten layers to thirty or forty. And sometimes shapes appear; in the case of this painting, a tiny buddha seemed to materialize once I stepped back to look at it, for which I have no explanation. These pieces seem to emerge from the field of practice; then I return them to the field of practice. It's as though these recent works are emerging from silence as a humble offering of my practice to whoever resonates with the work."

I think back to when I used to paint just for fun—always painting the faces of Eastern monks and women immersed in prayer. There is something unsettling about the creative process: Perhaps we are never truly able to bring to life what we envision. At least for me, I have always had vivid, beautiful visions, yet translating them into art—whether through painting or writing—was often accompanied by deep frustration. At times, the longing to communicate the beauty of what I felt even brought me sadness because it seemed impossible to do so fully.

Now, with a different perspective, I believe that facing whatever arises during the creative process—any form of self-expression through art—can ultimately lead us to the Divine because we recognize that we are not the ones truly creating, although we are blessed to experience the fruits of creation. Creativity offers bold alternatives, making change and transformation exciting in a deeply divine way. Through creativity, we can reach the parts of ourselves that don't yet shine, the parts that haven't been touched by light, but we can also let manifest and express the beauty of being immersed in silence and presence. Probably the best works of art come from that place: not from craving for forms and meanings but from having let it all go.

When in a creative flow, we can move beyond black-and-white thinking and bring our own colors to the picture. While the goal of spirituality isn't to expand our imagination, we can use the qualities of the mind and heart—including imagination—to work in our favor. We can bring everything into the vast reservoir of our search for truth. Every part of us is needed to fully experience the sacred.

***Both as individuals and as a collective, we are facing immense challenges globally. How can we keep an open heart and a spacious mind as we navigate these times?***

"Practice," Elena says. "Practice is my priority, now that I've seen how it's changed how I see, move, speak, and learn. Morning sitting practice happens at Upaya most days; sometimes I sit in the evenings at home as well. During practice periods, I'm there all month, in the Zen schedule; it can be medicinal for me to drop it all and just surrender to the rigor and timing of things.

"There's a poem I really love from *Cultivating the Empty Field* by Taigen Dan Leighton called "Song of the Grass-Roof Hermitage" by a Chan ancestor from eighth-century China that opens my heart every time I read it, so I read it often. It reminds me to let go, to relax, to open my hands, to respect the teachings, and to stay in practice.

"We're being invited to turn within, to let go of opinions, habit energies, and beliefs and to practice coming fresh to each moment as it arises. If we can actually let go of all that isn't the present moment and open our hands and walk, innocent, we become able to receive reality as it is, with less resistance. We can be a source of untangling the myriad challenges of our time, rather than worsening the tangle in which we find ourselves."

The end of our conversation brings me back to a time many years ago. It was a rainy morning at the Buddhist monastery of Chithurst in England. We were in the final month of a silent winter retreat. I walked through the wet grass on my way to the meditation hall. A question arose within me: If I were to die today, would I be ready to let everything go? The answer came instantly—yes. Despite my young age, my life had been so full and intense that it felt complete.

A few minutes after settling onto my meditation cushion, behind a row of monks whose shaved heads were all I could see, an unbearable pain spread through every part of my body. It came out of nowhere, as if all the suffering of the universe had suddenly poured itself into the vessel of my being in a single instant. I felt my life force draining away, slipping from my body like a fluid. *This is dying*, I suddenly recognized. *The body is about to be left behind.*

Panic surged—boundless, all-consuming. But then, a wiser voice stepped in and asked, *Who is dying?* This was the core question of the Theravada teachings I had been so deeply immersed in. I knew the correct answer—no one dies—but at that moment, I also knew that I didn't truly know it. The realization wasn't mine; I didn't embody it. It was just an idea I had encountered and adopted. The doors to the deathless—to what doesn't die in ourselves—remained closed to me. And so, I would truly die.

In that timeless moment, I understood—life must be spent cultivating awareness as if it were the greatest of all riches, in every given moment, while walking, speaking, and eating, so that when the moment comes to face the unknown, one is ready. You really don't want to get there fully unprepared!

When the bell rang, I was pulled back into the world of the living.

To embrace death means to draw ever closer to the sacredness of each moment, found precisely in its unfolding within change, in its being an unrepeatable composition of converging factors. My mother, who is almost seventy, confessed to me that she and her friends now think about death every night. To them, it's a gloomy thought, but actually, it's illuminating! We must make space for it. Death is a reality that holds immense potential for awakening. As women we tend to conceal every trace of our natural aging until the very last moment. But our bodies are speaking to us: *You won't always be strong and healthy, so you shall learn to be soft because you'll get vulnerable*, they remind us. *I will carry you only so far, so you shall learn to see beyond me.* And we must be honest about this.

I see old age as a powerful phase for women, a time when women could embody wisdom—simply because they have lived fully till that point. Yet so often, they don't. They fear losing what they have. They fear getting sick and dying in pain. They believe beauty is entirely behind them. And if an inner vision has not been cultivated, what remains? But if we allow life to teach us—through its cycles and phases—we arrive prepared for the moment of leaving the body, the most natural thing in the world.

Cherishing the gift of the body and the heart-mind and honoring our relationships as fully as possible prepare us to learn, again and again, life's greatest lesson: letting go so that only love remains. As you let go, you move into a space of surrender and a space in which you don't hold anything. With a trusting devotion, knowing that the intelligence of life works for us 24/7 and brings the right challenges at the right time, we can place ourselves in service to awareness itself—offering our heart fully to whatever is here, as a silent act of love.

PART THREE

# Birth

WEAVING OUR WAY FORWARD

As we repeatedly embrace darkness and density, new spaces become available to us—spaces we never knew existed. The dark womb is illuminated, infused with the light of awareness. Losing the sense of control over life, we can finally dance in the darkness. Here life reveals itself as an indestructible force, beyond all dualities, to which only wild devotion can be an adequate response. Peace and compassion transcend death, guiding us toward rebirth into a new paradigm. We are granted a new vision—one that is whole, luminous, and unifying, where shadow and light cease to be opposites and become part of the same weaving.

In this final section, we encounter four women of unwavering presence—each guiding us toward a different kind of sacred rebirth.

Lama Tsultrim Allione, a pioneer of Tibetan Dharma in the West, author of *Women of Wisdom* and founder of the Tara Mandala Buddhist center in Colorado, reveals the spiritual roots of the environmental crisis. She challenges us to rethink the way most religious traditions perceive the earth, nature, and the feminine, urging us to reclaim the sacredness of the land and its resources. Can we be reborn, here and now, and forge new bonds of reverence with nature?

Antonella Lumini, a guardian of silence and urban hermit in the heart of Florence, speaks of how silence can transform your life. She unveils the face of God as Mother and invites us to be reborn in the Spirit—an essence that is, at its core, feminine.

Vanamali Mataji, Hindu master, reminds us that in India, all women are seen as living manifestations of the Divine Mother. She calls us to be reborn as devis, as goddesses—reclaiming the sacredness of our form and the sovereignty of our purpose.

Julia Watts Belser, rabbi and visionary, teaches us how to fracture limiting structures from within. From her, we learn to apply just the right pressure in just the right place—to crack the shell, to let the light flood in. And in that moment, we are reborn into something ancient, something that has always been waiting just beyond the veil, just a breath, just a shell away.

Sacred rebirth is about finding our bones holy—stepping into the temple of our body with a spirit renewed in joy, forgiveness, and playfulness.

And so, we step forward—not as seekers but as weavers of meaning welcoming within ourselves distant worlds. Even in the most shattered fragments, wholeness remains the unseen force that weaves everything together. And we are reborn into wholeness, again and again.

9

# Rebirthing the Divine Feminine

## LAMA TSULTRIM ALLIONE

The ecological crisis, including climate disruption, has roots in religious traditions that view the earth as something to exploit, with the Divine seen as transcendent, male, and separate from nature and women. This mindset has led us to neglect the earth as sacred. The fates of women and nature are deeply connected: What happens to one impacts the other. Until we challenge these ingrained beliefs, little will change.

—LAMA TSULTRIM ALLIONE

I met Lama Tsultrim Allione just after she finished leading a retreat on the Ground of Being. She welcomed me into her room, and I was struck by something about the way she sat. Barefoot, her feet looked like beautiful roots, adorned with a subtle anklet. Elegantly dressed in burgundy, there was something wild yet perfectly composed in her posture, a hint of the revolutionary work she has done over the decades to bridge the Eastern tradition of Tibetan Buddhism with

Western—particularly American—culture and to emphasize women's place in it. This is where I wanted to begin.

***You followed a female lineage, Machig Labdron, within a patriarchal tradition, and you brought to light stories and practices of Tibetan women saints in your book* Women of Wisdom. *How was it for you to do all of this as an American woman inside the Tibetan Buddhist culture? Was there an inspirational figure who motivated you to make these changes?***

"I started doing Machig Labdron's practices in 1973," Lama Tsultrim told me, "but I didn't know her biography. I discovered it when, in need of stories about women, I wrote *Women of Wisdom*. The book was born out of my own personal need, because I lost a daughter—she died of sudden infant death syndrome in 1980. At that time, I started to look for biographies of women, and I found Machig Labdron and the others I presented in *Women of Wisdom*. When I first started to look for those stories in Tibet, I would ask lamas and other people for stories of women teachers, and they'd look at me and say, 'We don't have that.' And then I'd say 'dakinis,' and they'd say 'Oh, dakinis, of course! There is Machig Labdron, Yeshe Tsogyal . . .' and they'd name three or four more. I realized that they didn't see ordinary women with that divine potential. You had to be a dakini, a demigoddess, which implies an enlightened feminine presence.

"It was an interesting process to find those biographies and to write about the women. It made me start to research women's spirituality in general. This was in the early 1980s. At that time there was a strong movement of women's spirituality in the United States and England. They were looking at how spirituality could or would be different for women, since all the main existing spiritual traditions were created by men and primarily for men. They were asking questions that I never thought of asking like, What would spirituality look like if it was created by women? So, that was also important for me—to discover the Western roots of the exploration of women in spirituality. Getting to know the work of Merlin Stone, Carol Christ, Marija Gimbutas, and Margot Adler, to name a few, and combining the Western approach to what I found in Tibet helped me to find my own way."

***What were your main discoveries around women's spiritual practice in Tibetan traditions?***

"Within the tantric tradition there are different levels for understanding the divine feminine," Lama Tsultrim explains. "There is the Great Mother, Prajnaparamita Devi, which is the primordial space of phenomena—formless, empty, and pure potentiality. It is feminine in the sense that it has the potential to give birth to the phenomenal world. In the Tibetan tradition it is symbolized by the primordial female buddha, Samantabhadri. She is the basic space, the Ground of Being, and she is naked because she is formless. And then Samantabhadra, the masculine counterpart, is the awareness that discovers that space and returns into union with it. They are portrayed as an image called the *yab-yum*, the union of male and female: She is the ground itself, and he is the awareness that discovers that ground. This is the dharmakaya level.

"Then we have the sambhogakaya, the dimension of luminosity that radiates from the dharmakaya. Here are the enlightened feminine energies that are not of this world, but they are in a dimension of luminosity: Tara, Vajrayogini . . . all the deities are there. They are the luminous expression of that Ground of Being. The level where we are is called the nirmanakaya, and we can perceive dakinis and beings who are embodied as humans. There are the historical women whom I researched and the many great women practitioners whose stories were never written. A more recent one is Sera Khandro, who lived in the early twentieth century and wrote her autobiography, which was rare. She was a *terton*, a treasure discoverer. It is very unusual that she would consider herself valuable enough to write her story, but she did. Her story is now in the process of being translated. Even today, there are still women who are teaching Dharma and are great yoginis."

Lama Tsultrim describes yab-yum—the sacred union of masculine and feminine principles in Tibetan Buddhism—as a symbolic expression of enlightenment. In this view, the female represents the ground of being or emptiness (*sunyata*), the vast, open space of ultimate reality. The male represents awareness (*rigpa*), the illuminating consciousness that recognizes and engages with that ground. Their union signifies the inseparability of wisdom (prajna) and compassionate action (*upaya*), essential for awakening. So, ultimately, we are that perfect union. We are used to thinking of ourselves as individuals rather than as the union of opposing cosmic principles that meet and merge within us.

***How can the practice of Dzogchen, the nonduality practice, help us in realizing that we are a union of all dualities?***

"There is a very beautiful teaching that says that the five *skandhas*, the constituents of a human being, are the five male buddhas, and the five elements are the five female buddhas," Lama Tsultrim says. "So, within our own bodies, these are in nondual union. The fire element in our body is in union with Amitabha, the male buddha connected with the fire element, the West, and so on.

"In Vajrayana Buddhism, we see the world as sacred. The world itself is the mandala. Within our own bodies we experience a state of nonduality of masculine and feminine independent from our gender. The other interesting thing about Vajrayana is that you might be a woman but during practice you might visualize yourself as a male, like Avalokiteshvara, for example. Or you might be a man doing the practice of Tara. For example, His Holiness the Dalai Lama does a lot of Tara practice, where he sees himself as Tara. There is a natural gender fluidity in Vajrayana. We don't think of ourselves as fixed with one gender or the other, but we might experience ourselves as having a different gender or as a union of both in order to manifest certain inner qualities. Sometimes you visualize yourself as masculine and feminine in union, both at the same time."

***Can we say that, independently from gender, there is a need to reconcile with the sacred feminine within us?***

"I believe that there is a need for a relationship with the sacred feminine for both genders, or however you identify," Lama Tsultrim asserts, "because we don't live in a balanced situation in that regard. If you think about all the religions in the world, they are all predominantly male, and the divine aspect is anthropomorphized as a male. Men are controlling the religions, and men are controlling women's bodies within religions, so we need to bring forth the feminine, to invite her to the table and find her within ourselves.

"So far, I haven't had any women teachers. I have had the inspiration of Tara and the dakinis, but I didn't have a woman lama I could connect with. There are some, but I didn't have a connection with anyone. Also, some female lamas are so male identified, they act like the male lamas. We need to develop women teachers because they may embody the teachings in a slightly different way. We also need to find the presence of the feminine within ourselves, whether we are male or female, and bring that out, as historically the feminine leans toward peace and nonviolence because women create life. A woman who has had a baby knows how hard it is to raise a child and is going to be less likely to want to send any child into war. For example, His Holiness the Dalai Lama said that if we had more women in government, more women's views present at the table when important decisions are being made, we'd have a more peaceful world. We don't know if it's true or not because we haven't experienced it, but it sounds likely.

"Many women have been brought up within a patriarchy to the extent that, even though they have a woman's body, they aren't really representing the feminine outside of that patriarchal control and influence. As more women find their true voice, the situation might change. In this society, they think they have to be like men to succeed. But they don't need to be like men. They might ask themselves, *What's different about me? What are the different energies that I might have that could possibly be beneficial?*"

I discussed this same idea with Jetsunma Tenzin Palmo when she spoke about the importance of doing business in a feminine way. Women must not lose their feminine qualities on the path to success. Finding the expression of the divine feminine within each of us is key. Maintaining that connection is a way to remain anchored in our deepest authenticity and to achieve success without losing ourselves. It is a way to soar while staying rooted at the same time.

***What, in your experience, is the divine feminine?***

"It has different aspects," Lama Tsultrim says. "It's not only peaceful; there is also the wrathful or fierce feminine. In the Tibetan tradition, the fierce feminine is very important, and it has a protective quality, like a lioness protecting her cubs. Through practices, we can build a relationship with that through visualizations, allowing the blessings and energies from the lineages to come into us. When you perform a Tibetan practice, whatever it is, it's always within a lineage, and there are energies and blessings that are passed down through that. When you do a tantric practice, you embody the deity you are visualizing, and that process of embodiment has an impact on the body. These practices are a way to find a relationship with the sacred feminine. For example, the practice of Tara has twenty-one aspects—some are peaceful, some are wrathful. The twelfth Tara is for climate change.

This practice is about creating balance in the seasons, in the rains, and so on, which is historically her 'job.' The twenty-one Taras are a very good example of all the aspects of the feminine.

"I've done a lot of practice with the fierce lion-headed dakini who removes obstacles. One thing I've discovered—and others have had a similar experience—is that visualizing the fierce dakini and engaging in her practice brings me a deep sense of peace. Perhaps this is because it allows a repressed part of us to surface, granting it permission to exist in a transformed way, which in turn fosters a greater sense of inner peace. Even though she's fierce, instead of feeling more wrathful, we feel more peaceful."

I am happy to hear more about specific practices for integrating the sacred feminine, which feels like a continuation of ideas from Lama Tsultrim's book *Wisdom Rising: Journey into the Mandala of the Empowered Feminine*, a map for putting into practice this precious and essential integration of the sacred feminine. The mandala she describes in the book presents five aspects of the empowered feminine, mirroring the five wisdom dakinis (female embodiments of wisdom in Tibetan Buddhism). Each aspect represents a different wisdom energy that, when balanced, leads to transformation, healing, and empowerment. It is a response to both the historical suppression of feminine power and the need for an integrated spiritual path where women—and the feminine principle—are fully honored. I'm curious to know more.

***How can we work with the practices of the mandala of the empowered feminine that you share in your book* Wisdom Rising*?***

"The mandala of the empowered feminine is the mandala of the five dakinis," explains Lama Tsultrim. "At its center is a core space surrounded by the four directions, each associated with a specific emotional pattern—such as anger or jealousy—as well as its corresponding wisdom that emerges when that pattern is transformed. In this way, the very quality that seems to be a problem becomes a source of wisdom once the struggle around it is released.

"For example, the wisdom aspect of anger is clarity. When you are angry, there is a sharpness and precision to your perception that can be destructive if misused. But when the dualistic fixation—the inner struggle—is removed, what remains is pure clarity, which transforms into mirrorlike wisdom. Each of the five families—the center and the four directions—has both an encumbered emotional pattern and a wisdom quality connected to it. The mandala of the empowered feminine becomes fully activated when we step into that central space, engaging with all four directions through the transformed aspects of the five wisdoms."

Thanks to this guide, we can transform our most challenging emotions into wisdom—or rather, recognize the element of wisdom within them. If we find ourselves in a period of confusion and darkness, we can choose to stay with that confusion, welcome it, and observe it instead of immediately searching for an escape or an absolute answer. Perhaps, precisely from this acceptance and observation, an unexpected insight will arise, and we could experience the wisdom of absolute clarity. As women, we often let emotions take over. But if we allow them to be and look at them more deeply, we can gain from them—every time—a lesson in wisdom. Of course, many of us never learned this when we were young, and in daily life it's not always easy to apply, but it is revolutionary to learn this knowledge at any age.

***You are a mother and now also a grandmother. How has being a mother impacted your spiritual life, and how can a spiritual life guide the journey of motherhood? What would you suggest to mothers who are struggling to keep up with their spiritual practice?***

"I can totally identify with that struggle!" Lama Tsultrim exclaims. "Of course, there are no manuals; there are no books to guide us. Today there may be some teachers, but certainly there were none when

I was a young mother. Back then, the general reaction was 'Oh, now that you are going to be a mother, you have to stop your path.' I had to figure it out myself. It was a process for me to find the sacred in everyday life, and one of the ways I did that was by creating rituals.

"I created rituals with my children around meals—we always had a blessing, and each person would speak in a meaningful way before the meal. Of course, sometimes it was pure chaos, but most of the time we at least paused and had a moment of silence. Now my daughter has a mealtime ritual where each person answers these questions: What was the high point of your day? What was a challenge? What was an act of kindness that you did or observed today? Each person answers these questions and that creates a kind of ritual.

"I also transformed holidays by learning the ancient story connected to that holiday and celebrating by honoring that. Easter, for example, was originally connected to fertility. It's a spring festival, a rebirth celebration, thus the eggs and rabbits. Christmas is a solstice, so what we'd do was light a candle on the Christmas tree and write a prayer on a colored piece of paper, roll it, and tie it to the tree. I also created rituals for any time of change: If somebody was going away or coming back home, we'd have a ritual circle. My children have taken this into their lives and into their families. They also create rituals that have a deeper meaning.

"While my children were growing up, I tried to make time for myself to do short retreats, even just a weekend, to go away and do my deeper practices. At home, I continued to practice meditation, even with the kids crawling all over me! I remember when my two daughters were both little, and I was practicing, they'd literally tear down my shrine, and I'd be there meditating and thinking, *I'll fix it later*. I just let them be around me because my intention was not to create a separation. I didn't want them to feel alienated from it.

"I did a lot of things like this, finding my way as a mother. In Mahayana Buddhism, we talk about practicing for the benefit of beings, and we talk about compassion and giving up your own needs for others, but mothers do that all the time! And, in fact, they are used as an example in Mahayana teachings, where we're encouraged to try to develop love like a mother's. But the reality of that is very different from the theory. So, when you haven't had enough sleep and you are woken up again by your child, the reality of giving up your own needs is very different in that experience.

"I have practiced in a cave. I have practiced alone as a nun. Then I went almost directly into being a mother, and when I became a mother, all these things that I read about and studied I suddenly saw in a very different light. I realized this is what they meant when they talked about patience or giving up your own needs. *This* is what it really means!

"There were many things I thought I had overcome, but through motherhood I discovered I really hadn't. It was a real test to see honestly where I was in my spiritual path—to understand what I could cultivate in the cave but not in the kitchen. It was very humbling also because I just constantly made mistakes as a mother. You don't have training to be a mother, except from your own mother. I was lucky to have a wonderful mother, but often people don't have a mother or don't want to be like their mother. You have to figure it out by making mistakes and then trying to fix them.

"Having other women to talk to is vitally important. I was part of a women's circle, both in the United States and when I moved to Italy. We'd meet once a week, and it was very important for me to have that circle of other women to talk to. The first one I was in was a nursing group for breastfeeding. We'd talk about breastfeeding for about five minutes, and then everybody just wanted to talk about what was happening in their lives. We became very close. People went through amazing transformations in that group. One woman recognized she was gay; another went through an abortion. We went through so many things together."

***Something very powerful happens when women come together in this way. When we dare to be radically honest with each other and open, we become a network not only of support but also of deep transformation. It is almost as if our gathering is itself a superior force that enacts healing.***

"Yes, and men are scared about that!" Lama Tsultrim declares. "That's why, in some parts of the world, women's voices are actively suppressed. In the 1970s, an important part of the women's movement was women's circles. These circles are a very transformative opportunity."

***The active suppression of women in many places and the subtle oppression in others; economic, political, and social upheaval around the world; and the growing tumult of the very earth on which we rely are all showing us how something has gone astray with our understanding of our role as humans. How can we keep an open heart and a peaceful mind through all this? Is that the goal?***

"Everybody wants to be happy—even animals who simply want to live," Lama Tsultrim says. "We should remember this and help others find happiness, whether through small acts of kindness or larger systemic changes. The ecological crisis, including climate disruption, has roots in religious traditions that view the earth as something to exploit, with the Divine seen as transcendent, male, and separate from nature and women. This mindset has led us to neglect the earth as sacred. The fates of women and nature are deeply connected—what happens to one impacts the other. Until we challenge these ingrained beliefs, little will change. What religious values have contributed to the ecological crisis, and how might they be transformed to foster a worldview that honors the earth, fosters balance, and recognizes her as sacred?

"We must also continue to cultivate compassion and find ways to support those who are suffering, because there's more and more trauma that is happening, including climate trauma, war trauma, and so on. Meditation is an excellent tool to develop the wholesome inner qualities we will need to find ways to deal with all of this."

***Could we say that we need to balance the celestial side of spirituality with more body connection, with more grounding to this very sacred earth?***

"Yes," Lama Tsultrim agrees. "Buddhism also has a celestial dimension, but I think the modern split between spirit and matter has become problematic. There's a tendency to see spirit as superior to matter, as if we must rise above and escape the physical world to reach the spiritual. But in truth, matter is spirit as well. We don't have to leave—we can be fully present in our bodies and still be awake. Awakening isn't about going up and out somewhere; it's about being fully here, in presence."

***Matter feels slightly problematic to me. How can we embrace it? It is impermanent; it is a source of pain and death.***

"It's also so magical!" Lama Tsultrim insists. "When you look at a flower, a tree, the ocean, or anything in nature, it's unmistakably an expression of the Divine—a transmission of the sacred within matter. Think of the Native American teachings on daily gratitude for water, earth, wind, and all the elements we often take for granted or fail to see as sacred.

"As I mentioned, in Vajrayana, the five elements are seen as the five female buddhas, while the five skandhas, or aggregates, are the male buddhas—united within our own bodies. Viewing the earth as a female buddha, the ocean as a female buddha, fire as a female buddha, and so on, fosters a completely different relationship with the natural world. I wrote extensively about this in the beginning of *Wisdom Rising*, exploring how our political landscape is shaped by spiritual and religious values—and why shifting our perspective is so essential."

With a sense of purpose and urgency, our conversation ends, and I step out to the most gorgeous sunset melting into the landscape. Clearly the Divine is winking! It reaches my heart, and I'm filled with wonder and the depths of the conversation with Lama Tsultrim. With this conversation, another thread of women's spirituality is woven into place. This is not just a spiritual or environmental discourse; it is a matter of survival. Lama Tsultrim is living proof that the Divine can be brought into the material world. She herself acknowledged the challenges, yet this is the path. By supporting one another, practicing together, and sharing ways to integrate spirituality into family, work, and relationships, we can truly embody the divine feminine on earth. This is our mission. Giving up worldly life is not the only way. You can stay right where you are and change everything from within. Just as the sun sets and merges with the horizon, the divine feminine weaves itself into the fabric of existence, unseen yet ever-present, shaping life from within.

10

# Love Speaks Through Silence

## ANTONELLA LUMINI

When you know love because you experience it
by letting love love you, then you can also give it.

—ANTONELLA LUMINI

It is the first day of October. Passing over the Ponte Vecchio in Florence, I remember that I have been here before, though I cannot recall when. As I step onto the bus, I am slapped with a fine—not an unusual occurrence in Italy. Later, someone offers me a coffee, which is also very Italian. Finally, I reach Piazza Santo Spirito, a beautiful square. I see two women talking in front of a doorway; one of them must be Antonella. And indeed one of them turns and smiles at me, saying, "There she is!"

She greets me warmly, as if she has always known me. Carrying a bag stocked with vegetables, she seems to have just returned from the garden. There is nothing fancy about her appearance, but she radiates a striking brightness. She wears the simplicity of the countryside: a perforated cardigan and a long dark skirt, with her white hair pulled back at the nape of her neck. I help her with the shopping as she leads the way inside. The house we enter is one of those ancient palaces in the heart of Florence that exudes a fragrance of historicity, its stone edges smoothed by time.

It is immediately evident this is a house of contemplation. It embraces a central void—an inner courtyard abundant with vegetation. There are white chairs in the corridor between a bookcase full of mystical texts and a row of bright windows that overlook the courtyard. I pass a hall that is meant for group prayer, with wooden benches and a Tibetan bell, passing beneath the gaze of a number of smiling Madonnas. To me, a house only feels complete when it has a room for the Spirit. This one does: It is called a *poustinia*, a room for silence with a simple mattress on the floor, an Oriental rug, and a sober altar.

We sit on a white sofa in the living room, and I tell her about my project of gathering wisdom from women.

On hearing me, Antonella says, "These days, feminine energy must emerge. Spiritual energy is an antidote to the aggressive force that has taken over." In one sentence, it is as if she sums up the gist of my work. Her Tuscan accent adds a tinge of humor to even serious observations like this.

***You are described as an urban hermit. What does that mean to you?***

"They call me an urban hermit because I have long been known to walk a path of silence while living an apparently normal life in the city," Antonella says. "But I do not seek a label, an identification. The stereotypical image of the hermit on top of the mountain does not correspond to me and so, if anything, I feel like a guardian of silence. This is what emerged in the book I wrote with Paolo Rodari, *La custode del silenzio* [The guardian of silence], in which I first recounted my experience. However, I have been frequenting hermits for twenty years and, to tell you the truth, no one is the same as the other, and each one has its own story. So maybe I fit in too. In any case, the image of the hermit needs to be revised."

***Yours is a unique example of a life dedicated to the divine mystery outside of all structures and institutions. What can you say about your love affair with the unknowable, the indescribable? How did you become a guardian of silence?***

"My form of prayer is silence," Antonella tells me. "I discovered silence in 1980, at the age of twenty-eight. It was an extremely critical time in my life, for at the age of twenty-four, due to a surprising illness, I was given only a few years to live. The news was quite a jolt to me: I saw the face of death. I treated myself with a macrobiotic diet—which was considered crazy in those times—and it helped me to recover. Not soon after, however, I was once again thrown into the void. I had a terrible crisis and began to feel a strong call to be in solitude and silence. I used to walk around the Florentine hills and along the banks of the Arno to find peace. I felt in this silence an extraordinary joy that I had never known before. Perhaps it was similar to the joy of childhood—to that enchantment that you cannot identify as coming from anywhere in particular but that lends you a sense that you belong to the beauty of creation and are rooted deeply in it. It was like rediscovering the being that lives inside of me, like finding a precise new order. It was a great way of healing. This order enveloped me. I felt like I had so far been a dissonant note that was now being tuned. I received immense benefit from this, and it was no longer possible to return to the life I had lived before. I had to go against the tide. I loved silence and solitude, but I had not taken into account the loneliness that comes from not being understood. It was very painful."

***What does it mean to be a woman who discovers herself, who investigates the deep? A woman who steps out on her own into the unknown, in solitude and silence?***

"Initially, I wanted to hide myself," Antonella admits. "Even in the house, I would close the doors and windows. I made a red cross out of cardboard, and I would sit on the floor with a lighted lamp in front of that cross for days. When I told myself, *If I were to die now, I would feel an immense pain—a darkness—but I could stay in that pain,* that was big news for me. Earlier, I was running away from myself. Now, I could stay with what was there. Everything began to revolve around the silence.

"But I did not understand which way to go. I began to travel in search of my roots: to Greece, to Jerusalem, to the desert, to Egypt. I reread the epic poems, the Greek tragedies. While everyone went to India, I wandered around the Mediterranean. After five years of such wandering, one day I went out to buy a Bible. Hearing a priest speaking in a church, I realized that what I was looking for was the love of Christ that I had known as a child. In an instant, a touch in the soul provoked conversion. Thus began another pilgrimage because I felt like a fish out of water in the church environment.

"I began to frequent the Hermitage of San Pietro alle Stinche, founded by Father Giovanni Vannucci, a great enlightened man of our time, whom I got to know shortly before he died. It was at the Stinche that they told me about Monsignor Gino Bonanni, an elderly priest. He was a true man of silence, capable of listening, and he gave me a book to read: *Poustinia: Encountering God in Silence, Solitude, and Prayer* by Catherine de Hueck Doherty. I did not even know the language that the word *poustinia* belonged to but, as soon as I started reading the book, I realized that it corresponded to me. *Poustinia* means 'desert' in the Russian language and alludes to a vocation to be in silence in the Orthodox tradition. One might well say that it is in continuity with the call of the Desert Fathers and Mothers—a call to live in silence in the freedom of the Spirit—without preestablished rules, without having to be accountable to anyone, without having to be institutionalized in a monastery. It is a form of letting oneself be carried.

"The more one enters into the mystery of God's silence, the more one opens oneself to listening to human beings. For me, it was like that—it was completely natural for me to open myself up to listening to people. I spent more than thirty years in seclusion while living a seemingly normal life. I worked in the National Library during the day and then there were long, dark nights when I did not understand where I was going. I was looking for someone to understand me, and I would sometimes fear that I had made a mistake; for I had not married, I was not in a loving relationship, and I had not entered the monastery. I spent long hours—sometimes whole days—in that interiority, listening to the silence. My refuge, however, was the Hermitage of Cerbaiolo near La Verna, toward Arezzo. It was founded by Chiara, a lay nun who devoted herself to her goats. She was a great figure, a true contemplative, who was particularly active, intuitive, courageous, determined, and full of energy. Here, there was a small hermitage in the forest without light or water—almost like a cave that clung to a spur of rock. For me it was the place for inner listening, a descent into hell that would strip you of everything."

*What does inner listening consist of?*

"It means to prepare oneself to bring forth what lies deep within," Antonella explains. "The path of interiority requires an inner struggle. Early monasticism places the inner struggle at the center, as the way of purification. Inner experience lays one bare and brings to the surface what the soul hides—including our ancient history, which also concerns our genealogical inheritance. Souls have a bearing that comes from afar. Christian salvation is primarily a way of healing the psychic reality, and it begins in the here and now of our everyday life. The Holy Spirit works in the soul to release fears and dissolve darkness and selfishness. Everything must be healed. All blocked energy must be brought back to the flow. Our being needs to be healed by reentering those emotions that remain within and letting them emerge to be purified by the loving action of the Holy Spirit. This is what is meant by the resurrection of our bodies. It begins here. The more that a purified and pacified life conforming to the measure of love takes shape in us, the more the spiritual life within us awakens."

I am truly shocked that, for more than thirty years, Antonella found no one with whom she could share this intense experience. In many of my conversations, community is an important part of the spiritual journey, especially communities of women. I want to better understand how it was possible for her to wait, quietly, keeping everything personal and internal for so long before pulling back the veil with the publication of her book *La custode del silenzio* in 2016.

***In all those years prior to the publication of your book, did you have no spiritual friends with whom you could connect? Did you advance your spiritual practice in perfect solitude?***

"That's right," Antonella says. "I was often misunderstood, but something within was holding me. The experience of the Spirit is a living wisdom. It teaches; it accompanies. It rises within like a master, an inner teacher. See that fresco of the Trinity? The Holy Spirit is depicted in a feminine way. The Holy Spirit is the motherly face of God. I wrote a book on this called *Dio è madre* [God is mother]. When I came back to Christianity, I discovered a completely different God from the one I had known before—one with a love that embraces you and carries you, one in whom you can entrust yourself—the consoler, as the evangelist John called it. He certainly does not allude to any consolation offered by the world but rather to the consoler who fills you with love.

"The consoler brings to you that inner fullness that becomes like a pin that holds you. Though we all often flutter, there is a pin that holds us. I think that is what held me. I could not betray it. Contact with pure love, as the French philosopher Simone Weil says, is like a touch that is imprinted on the soul. In those lonely years, the words of Weil were a great traveling companion for me, along with the books of Father Vannucci and the mystics."

After so much care, it is no wonder that the fruits falling from Antonella's white tree are golden. If you open them, you find the seeds of an immense act of faith that was required for her to advance into the invisible. Antonella followed her feelings to the very end and allowed herself to be guided along a road that was neither written about nor indicated by any external support. Her experience is living proof of how that inner connection—when it reaches a certain intensity—can lead us unerringly forward in an integrated way that is reflected in our body, our habits, and our choices.

Life bends or positions itself—with gratitude and intelligence—to serve this inner force that knows. As it is tested, the power of the invisible inevitably reveals itself. If we can turn our branches and leaves inward, we might find the sun within as Antonella did. Her mode of prayer and way of life sprang from the full emptiness of silence. I am left with one small question, however. I look at her beautiful, clear and open face, which reminds me of a spring moon. I imagine her as a young woman, so graceful and full of ardor and courage.

***In all this, has the desire to experience human love—to have a partner—simply taken a back seat?***

"Not at all," she says. "In fact that was a great struggle for me. At the time I discovered silence, I had a boyfriend, but there was no future for us. We would be together for three days, and then I would want to be alone for a week. I could not give up the silence. At some point, I realized that this could not go on. He was not suited for that kind of life. It was a very painful separation. However, I thought that maybe in the future I could meet someone who was sensitive to spirituality. It seemed to me that every now and then I would see a halo on someone's head, but they were all straw fires. What mattered to me was a spiritual affinity. I had changed inside, and I could not compromise on essential things.

"Eros is a divine force, but it is about lack—a lack of love that wants to be filled. In contemplation, eros is filled, because the soul is always overflowing. We do not ordinarily have the capacity to experience the intensity of pure beauty which, when it appears, is like a miracle, a marvelous thing. You look at a sunset, you look at a tree, and you feel a strong vibration that you cannot contain. The soul dilates. This is a fundamental exercise that pacifies the being. Only the fullness that the contemplative life gives can satiate the real need—the need for beauty, for light—and only then can eros be transformed into *agape*, or selfless love.

"Agape must be ardent. Creation is erotic—alive and overflowing. When we connect with it, we feel its vibration, its energy in motion. This fills us deeply; it is ecstasy. One is beyond oneself because everything is within—completely absorbed. It is an ecstatic stillness, a fullness in which nothing is lacking. And from that fullness, something overflows.

"The usual demons—passions, possessiveness, and attachments—are there. It is better not to fight evil, but to grow the goodness in us. If you feed the good, the demon diminishes and becomes more containable. If you fight it, you give it strength, and you fail because it is a collective spiritual force. When good arises, it takes everything else away.

"For Jews, eternal life is linked to the transmission of life through descendants, through genealogy. But Jesus appears without a wife or children—a striking departure from this tradition. What does this signify? It carries a powerful message.

"God created man in His image, meaning that human beings inherently strive for wholeness—first by integrating the masculine and feminine within themselves and second by harmonizing the physical, psychic, and spiritual dimensions of their being. If we focus on Jesus's revolutionary message, whether he had a wife or not is ultimately irrelevant. What matters more is the transformation of eros into agape that he embodied. Spiritual fullness springs from the connection with the Father because only the consciousness of belonging to the divine life can fill us. Then, you have love to give—a love that is free from attachment and possessiveness—a love that can pour itself out to all. It is born of spiritual maternity and paternity together."

*From eros to agape—I still have a long way to go*, I think to myself. I have a weakness for men with a halo, but I am trying to quit this habit. I tell Antonella about the three-month, silent winter retreat I attended for two consecutive years when I lived with Theravada monks. I lived at the edge of the forest, in a wooden *kuti*, or hut, with a stove and nothing more than the essentials. No phone, no laptop, no books, nobody to talk with. After a month of silence, I was beginning to go mad. At the same time, I fell in love with a man in robes. (Perhaps the two phenomena are related.) I adored his open heart and the gentleness of his manner. I was committed to silence but stole a few exchanges of words from under the rigors of practice.

I kept passion at bay and tried to turn it inward. I almost enjoyed burying myself in the fermenting density and muck of my inner states. I came to weep over many infinitesimal things. Often, in that state, a breakthrough would eventually open me up, and I would find myself holding a treasure of treasures. An inner blossoming would unfold, releasing the fragrance of an incredible essence. I saw the diamond light of awareness. And yes, it was perfect. For a time, I would exist in a state of completeness.

But then, the weeds would push their way through, leaving gaps and bringing with them the familiar sense of separation and the longing to fill it. That was the way. That was how I moved through the days, the weeks, the months—burning through brambles and inhaling openings. Sinking and reemerging, caught between painful chaos and silence. Casually and madly falling in love with someone I couldn't even talk to.

Hearing this, Antonella says, "In the Christian way, in the love of Christ, solitude becomes an inhabited solitude. The world is in great need of silence! It is absurd that certain ways find references only in the Eastern tradition. The great potential of the Christian tradition must be reactivated by reviving and passing on the experience of silence. This is why we founded the association Pustinia-Italia: precisely to offer people the possibility of living the experience of silence independently. Being in the middle of nowhere is a great test, for you are confronted by fears. Spiritual life requires coming face-to-face with the mystery that contains us, like the Desert Fathers and Mothers who did not know what awaited them, who had no rules."

***Can you talk more about the experience of silence? What kind of tale does silence tell? What message survives in the intensity of silence? How does our gaze change when contemplating the great mystery in silence?***

"Contemplation leads us to wisdom," Antonella replies. "Reality consists of both the visible and the invisible, the knowable and the unfathomable. The soul is drawn to the invisible, and we cannot suppress this deep yearning. Nourishing the soul is not optional; it is essential.

"When we contemplate the beauty of creation, we come into contact with the uncreated. Contemplation isn't a detached act of observation, as if we are separate from what we see. Rather, it is an interactive, immersive experience where we are taken in. The contemplative gaze is always overwhelmed, unable to fully contain the beauty it encounters. Yet, over time, it is purified, as beauty seeps in, revealing the divine order that underlies all things. The invisible then shines through the visible. One must allow this expansion; otherwise, the soul withers.

"What we contemplate shapes us. If we are constantly absorbed in our smartphones, we conform to them, learning their language, and eventually, we feel a soul-level anguish, a kind of depression. The word *anguish* comes from the word *angustus*, meaning 'narrow' or 'prison.' But contemplation activates a different kind of language—the language of the Spirit.

"When we taste the beauty of creation and feel its deep resonance, it aligns us with the divine order. It awakens a force that penetrates us deeply and acts within us. When we enter silence, all the inner disorder we carry rises to the surface, like uncorking a bottle of sparkling champagne—our thoughts, anxieties, and negativities bubble up. The turbulence of the world is always with us, which makes finding balance through silence even more urgent.

"Mystery reveals itself in traces that transform our way of seeing. Feeling becomes wisdom. Contemplating the mysteries of faith is essential, even though they transcend what the mind can grasp. We say we believe in the Divine, but what do we actually believe in?

"When we contemplate mysteries like the incarnation, the transfiguration, the resurrection, or Jesus walking on water, we engage with dimensions that are invisible but still exert a force. They are alive; they are memorials, as Jewish tradition describes them. To contemplate them is to enter into a relationship with their vibration, to taste them in some way. Through this, mystery—the spiritual reality—begins to reveal itself."

***What emotional burdens and challenging legacies does a woman inevitably encounter on the path of self-discovery, simply by virtue of being a woman? And conversely, what limitations does she not have?***

"Let's start with the ones she has," Antonella suggests. "I personally felt a lot of resistance during this journey. I saw no role models. I used to ask myself, *Have I become a spinster?* I wondered if I was doing everything wrong. It was a struggle within me. I understood the world's incomprehension, but I did not yet understand myself. When spiritual reality begins to take hold, it takes you on its path, it conforms you to itself, you become different from others, and it can be painful.

"I believe I have traveled a very feminine path, which began with illness. The body has been central in my experience. It is important to value the body that, as Saint Paul says, is the 'temple of the spirit.' It is a gift that is given to us. It is sacred. In this respect, Mary is a real force, for she is the bearer of a new vision of the feminine. The processes of concealment, keeping silent, welcoming, and carrying everything in the heart—these are typical elements of the feminine. Caring, giving birth, and midwifing the death process are the original orbits in which the feminine archetype acts. These are the fundamental dimensions of which women have been dispossessed. Today, we are born, cared for, and die in hospitals, outside of the orbit of loving care. How can we recover these domains, live them, and make them come alive? Emancipation is sacrosanct; it is important that women have made their voices heard. But being mostly absorbed in the male reality, at work and in institutions, they risk conforming to male behavior and betraying themselves.

"My path has given me the opportunity to experience gratuitous love—spiritual motherhood—by caring for those around me and thus to rediscover and experience the original values of the female archetype. First, the female archetype must be healed by remaining in the gestation of the Spirit which, for me, is feminine. In Hebrew, Ruah—the Spirit—is feminine. Spirit is life-giving. I have long felt that the age of the Spirit has begun, and it is our work to expand mercy and love. We are all in this gestation of the Spirit—in a womb that generates love, that cares and grows. When you know love because you experience it by letting love love you, then you can also give it. Today, few have this kind of love to give. We must go back and tap into the source."

***Since the feminine is an archetype, does that mean both men and women need to recover it? Can we say that women have moved away from their center toward the masculine—to gain something that was missing—and now they can afford to return to live in the power of their center?***

"It is true that women have always been oppressed," Antonella agrees, "but, in the background, the feminine world was very powerful—and the male world also rested on it. Women were deeply connected to one another and shared strong solidarity. Now that the hidden world of women has disappeared—it disintegrated with the advent of the industrial age—women have stopped working in the home, in the fields, and have entered the world of work ruled by male power. We must return to the original archetype so that, once activated, it not only influences every woman but also catalyzes transformations in men.

"The idea of the sacred family itself is a revolutionary model. It envisions a putative father—one who renounces possession of his wife and children and is no longer bound solely by blood ties. It proposes a perspective in which every child, as a child of God, is entitled to receive both maternal and paternal care. In this vision, I see the emerging horizon of the human family. The holy family is not the idealized, picture-perfect family portrayed in the Mulino Bianco [Italy's top bakery brand] Italian biscuit advertisements. Instead, it represents a true leap in consciousness.

"The virgin mother symbolizes the purity of heart—a mother who prioritizes her child's fulfillment over her own attachment. At the wedding in Cana, Mary initiates her son Jesus into his mission. She knows it is dangerous, yet she urges him to go. These are the models that guide us, but they must be read and interpreted with understanding.

"Even today's extended families—when they succeed in fostering relationships of mutual benevolence—represent a step forward. What matters most is not to betray love. A separation or division should not turn love into hatred but rather transform it into new forms of mutual friendship and goodwill. This, I believe, is the horizon we should strive for. It is not about rigid roles but about the possibility of transforming love."

***Can we see silence as a means of making space for the Word of God?***

"Yes, it is exactly like that," says Antonella. "The Word of God is a creative act. It is imprinted on us, as every personal life springs from this creative act. But what does it mean to realize the Word of God in one's life, to actualize the creative act that gave birth to us? In Christ, we see the answer. We see the fullness of humanity—human beings capable of giving love freely. This is the goal.

"It is a call, an impulse within us, and it is important to listen to it. The Word makes itself heard; it leaves its living imprint. Those who are listening for it hear the call, heed it, and take it seriously. You, too, are among those who have listened—you allowed yourself to be taken. Such a young girl—it truly gives hope!"

I am not really that young, I think. I am in my late twenties and already have quite a bit of white hair hiding amid the dark. But it is, of course, relative, and Antonella's enthusiasm rubs off on me. It is she who gives me hope. I thank her from the bottom of my heart for this wonderful meeting, and I tell her that I would like to stay a few more days in Florence to finish writing this book. She tells me to stay there in her house, as she is leaving for some time. I don't quite know what to say. This house is a dream, imbued with silence and sacred icons, Hebrew prints and antique chairs. It also feels like a blank canvas—spacious, clear, and bright. She encourages me to stay as long as I want. In the spirit of sisterhood, I accept. She briefly shows me around and gives me the keys.

When I return here the next day, to this house charged with silence, my inner struggle begins. On this path—when we release the burdens that naturally arise when looking within, with the help of divine love—the inner struggle disarms us, for it is a struggle that leads to surrender. Usually we move through life armed—as in a state of war—feeling that we must fight for peace. The intelligent commitment we can make is choosing disarmament: to make peace with war and the demons. To make friends with the terror. To care for the wounded parts within us that wander in search of relief. To enlarge the hospitality of our home toward infinity, so that there are no more internal or external enemies.

While leafing through her books, in the dim light of her home, I came across one of Antonella's poems in her book *Dio è madre*—just a few lines that seemed to contain everything. Having grown up reciting the Lord's Prayer, I was immediately struck by this poem dedicated to the Divine Mother, as it felt like the perfect feminine counterpart to the much-revered prayer. The lightness, sweetness, and grace of this poem make it a perfect prayer through which to address the Divine Mother, in harmony with Her intrinsic qualities:

Madre Nostra (Our Mother)
Who art the womb of life,
The Holy Spirit pours forth,
Love flows,
Bright beauty flourishes,
As in heaven so on earth.
Each day you nourish us with your grace.
You dissolve our closures.
Wrap us in the wonder
Of your creative work.
You preserve the memory of light
Even when we are in darkness
And free us from fear.

Every time we connect with that sense of belonging to the Divine within us, every time we let go and allow ourselves to be inhabited by it, we are reborn into our true nature as children of the Divine Father and the Divine Mother. It is the Spirit that cares for us, guiding our growth into awareness.

There will be an emptying. A space made available to us, free to inhabit.

And in that space, there will be a filling and a becoming—of beauty, harmony, and order. There will be a silent rebirth. Many ancient truths will be reborn along with us. There will be holy water all around and the ancient sacred names will begin to flow once again into the stream of extraordinary everyday life.

11

# You Are the Goddess and the Temple

## VANAMALI MATAJI

> In Hinduism, all women are sacred. In ancient times, the name Devi was added to each woman's name. . . . *Devi* means "goddess," and every woman is considered an aspect of the Divine Mother.
>
> —VANAMALI MATAJI

When I was in Rishikesh, India, confused and uncertain, healing in the Ganges River and asking the universe for guidance, somebody told me of a woman I should visit named Vanamali Mataji. "She has an ashram, and dresses only in lilac," they said. Lilac is the color of Krishna, the deity to which Mataji has dedicated her life. Her own spiritual name, Vanamali, is another name for Krishna. It means "one who wears a garland of wildflowers." A philosophy graduate and mother of two, Devi Menon (her birth name) received "the call" to set off on a pilgrimage to the Himalayas in search of a guru at age forty-six. In time, this choice, and this guru, would transform her life.

Vanamali Mataji's ashram in Tapovan, Rishikesh, enjoys an advantageous position overlooking the Ganges. From the terrace, one cannot see the havoc of buildings that have been compulsively crammed into every square foot of Rishikesh. From here, it is still possible to breathe in the glow of the ancient rishis, enlightened masters who have energetically held this land over the centuries.

Mataji's ashram is her spiritual home, but it has a distinctly domestic feel. It is open to anyone who wants to rest in silence or sing a holy chant and pray together. A gift of intimacy, Mataji is like a mother who extends a welcoming embrace to anyone who is intrigued or drawn to the spiritual. At the entrance, I am greeted by Brahmachari Mohan—a distinguished, sober, and devout Indian who never says anything more than is necessary and who, I later discover, is also the ashram's handyman and Mataji's cousin.

Mataji grabs her meditation cushion—which is also lilac—and smiles at me. A great pantheon of deity statues stands behind her, as well as myriad framed photos of masters and teachers whom she holds in her heart. I see Yogananda, Papaji, Babaji, Adi Shankaracharya, Anandamayi Ma, Mata Amritanandamayi, Sri Ramakrishna Paramahamsa, Swami Vivekananda, Swami Sivananda Saraswati, Papa Ramdas, Shirdi Sai Baba, and Neem Karoli Baba. The altar overflows with statues, incense, and a spirit of transcendence. You can feel the richness of her Hindu spiritual heritage—all the grace of the garlands of sages, all the power of their transmission—and the responsibility now falls on us to cherish and honor that legacy. The Divine overflows everything in this space, without exception. It is especially present on the altar, where a candle is lit beside a few rose petals, where God is evoked and recalled daily, and where even the children come, at the evening puja, for the ceremony of light.

Vanamali Mataji is incredibly vital and active. She has written numerous books and has an active social media presence with tens of thousands of followers. When I learn that she is eighty-two years old as we meet, I am pleasantly surprised—perhaps meditation promotes antiaging after all! Mataji chants a short prayer—almost everything in India begins with an Om—and we start with the sacred feminine.

***Can you tell me about the forms of the sacred feminine in the Hindu tradition and how they inspire you in everyday life?***

"In Hinduism, all women are sacred," Mataji answers. "In ancient times, the name Devi was added to each woman's name. For example, if she is named Kalyani, then her name becomes Kalyani Devi. This custom still survives in the villages. *Devi* means 'goddess,' and every woman is considered an aspect of the Divine Mother. Because every woman is part of the Divine Mother, they therefore must also be looked after. The many taboos related to women are not meant to cut them down or to diminish them but rather to protect them because it is well known that the woman is the womb of the world. Without her, there are no people in the world, so she must be protected.

"For example, during her menstrual period, a woman was not allowed to do any work. She had to rest completely from all things that might cause fatigue. She would stay quietly in her room, and food would be brought to her so that she could regenerate. It was as if, during those days when her womb was cleansing itself, she was preparing herself for another new life to come. The arrival of Western ideas threw another light on the matter, and Indian women began to feel limited by these customs. But originally such measures were taken for their health because it is necessary for a woman to have a healthy body and a healthy womb to accommodate a healthy life, so there was a hyperprotective tendency toward women.

"Another aspect was that of work in the house. Women ruled in the house; they worked in the fields around the house, taking care of the animals and the children. Now women must go to work immediately after having delivered a baby. You have some weeks or a month off, and then again you are pushed into this stream of work, and your child ends up in the hands of someone else who takes care of it. It used to be important for children to be brought up by their mother's love and care because the best formula is made by nature herself. It was fundamental for the culture. The restrictions in which the woman lived were a function of the well-being of the coming generation that came through her."

I understand her argument, but I can't help but wonder about the many women who sacrificed themselves and their dreams in the name of the family. And while the intention to protect and revere might have been the goal at one point, I know that in many parts of this beloved land of India, women are not treated with such kid gloves today. During their periods, most are put in a room outside their home and are not allowed access to temples because they are considered unclean. They generally don't receive favorable treatment. I ask Mataji about this.

"Temples are places where the pranic current is very active," she says. "This current allows our mind and energies to ascend to the higher chakras. When we go to the temple at times when the pranic current—called *prasoothi*—is active within us, we establish an opposing and descending force which, according to our sages, could cause infertility, endometriosis, tubal blockage, and other problems. This is one of the scientific reasons why menstruating women, and women who are pregnant beyond the eighth month, are forbidden to go to temples or places of worship. Our ancient taboos against entering temples had nothing to do with the desecration of divinity or the impurity of women—they were intended as a protection for women's health.

"I am sure that ignorant men, who knew nothing about our ancient culture, took this opportunity to suppress and control women, but the original reason was well-intentioned. In fact, we have always worshipped God in the form of women. We have an infinite number of goddesses in our pantheon. Even when a goddess is related to her male counterpart, her name always comes first: Lakshmi/Narayana,

Gauri/Shankar, Radha/Krishna. Her name comes first, because she is the Shakti; she is the power."

The word that I have heard spoken the most often since I arrived in India—except perhaps *laddus*, the highly addictive sweet balls made from dates, seeds, and coconut that yoga practitioners love—is *Shakti*. Women especially seem to love the word *Shakti*, speaking it in a tone of reverence as they experience the wonder of reclaiming something they do not know how they have lived without. Whenever a woman here is a bit on edge, she sings or puts on a long skirt and a pair of dangling silver earrings and says that she is drawing in Shakti—her female power. But Shakti is so much more than that.

"Shakti is the spark that starts the engine," Mataji continues. "The engine is Shiva. There is a beautiful conversation between [Shakti as] Parvati and Shiva. Parvati was doing *tapas* [austere practices] to win Shiva's love, and he told her, 'I am complete in myself; I do not need anybody.' To this, she replied, 'No, you need me. Without my power, you cannot achieve anything in this world.' Feminine power is very important. Without Shakti, all of creation would not even have started. All of nature is her form—it is her display of forms, for the enjoyment of the supreme Shiva. This is also depicted in the incredible image of [Shakti as] Kali dancing on Shiva's seemingly dead body. Shiva, without Shakti, is only *shava*—a corpse! This is an example to show that the male is powerless without the female Shakti! Such was the importance given to women throughout our history and mythology."

***Are Shiva and Shakti always united?***

"In the Skanda Purana," Mataji replies, "we find that the masculine and feminine are eternal principles involved in the projection of the universe. They are never separate and are fundamentally one—like gold and the ornament made from it. Shiva is inert consciousness; Shakti—without Shiva—is unconscious action. That is why Shakti is maya, an illusion. But maya also offers us pleasure, colors, music, and beauty. She brings joy into this life. For example, all arts and sciences come from her, in the form of Saraswati. Saraswati is not a male god; she is a goddess. She is also the goddess of learning, to whom the children pray so they can learn better."

Mataji's teachings flow from one topic to the next, connecting distant concepts like a river connects the mountains to the sea. Shakti (the feminine force), maya (illusion and pleasure), and Saraswati (the goddess of music and learning) are all under the same roof, are all fingers of the same hand. The force of life, primarily giving, abounds in an infinite richness of forms to give us the gift of illusion. Truth is covered by maya's veil. On one side, we fall into the perfect net of that illusion, and on the other side, it gives us the very chance to awaken. Like the mother who gave us birth. She's allowed us to come into being, but what we do with life is up to us. So it might be that the Divine Mother, as the infinite womb of the unknown that supports us, gives birth to us in this world so that we may grow beyond it.

I wonder what this world is about then.

***Is the world a kindergarten where we will remain until pain spurs in us the desire to pierce the veil and transcend the limits so that we may become aware of life in a more honest way? Is the Supreme Mother infinitely kind because she gives us a chance to regain the unity that we do not remember having lost? And what about the Divine Father?***

"Shiva is an aspect of Brahman, the formless, actionless witness," Mataji answers. "Brahman is the stage on which Shakti plays. Without the stage, there is no *lila*."

I had recently attended a Vedic philosophy lecture and recalled that Brahman is the absolute, uncreated, eternal, infinite foundation, source, and origin of all things. Shakti is Brahman's first emanation of power; she is the creative aspect of Brahman. Through her, the one becomes the many. She is the womb of the universe. Lila is the resulting "world effect"—the playground of divine energy that we perceive as the stage of our daily life.

"The education of children begins as early as the first month of life when they are in the womb," Mataji continues. "There is a Upanishad entirely dedicated to the womb—the *Garbha Upanishad*—that is thousands of years old and explains how the fetus grows. They already knew it at that time! They were already talking about the sperm entering the egg. If the role of the woman is diminished, then it is only because there is a profound ignorance about her fundamental role in creation. Without the woman, life does not go on."

***More and more women are releasing suppressed anger toward men. How can we manage and transform these emotions into love, understanding, and compassion, while also transforming ourselves from victimhood to freedom?***

"This is only possible through knowledge," affirms Mataji. "Everything is caused by ignorance. Men must be educated to understand the crucial role that women play in life as creatrices. Without them, there would be no creation. Your Western men must be reeducated to recognize women as divine."

I feel perplexed by her answer, and Mataji senses this. Sure, Western men need to rediscover the divine side of women—no doubt. But it is not as if Indian men are any better off. They may grasp the divine aspect of women, but many still do not respect women as emancipated persons.

"Emancipation from what?" Mataji asks me. "I am always surprised by that. We can never have equality with men. That is not what we want! It is absurd. Why are we asking for equality? We are far superior," she says, giving in to unrestrained laughter.

I get her point, but I have the impression that we are simplifying a very complex discourse. I am sure Mataji knows very well what she is talking about and does not underestimate the treatment women have received over the past centuries—and still do even today. Emancipation does not imply equality but a liberation from the prejudices and conditionings that limit women's autonomy and freedom. I consider that I may lack the tools to understand her point of view fully, so I decide to come at this from a different angle, and I ask her about surrender, the ability to give oneself completely to the Divine.

"Surrender can only happen through bhakti, devotion," she says. "You can surrender to God only if you have the deepest love for Him. Only then does your ego subside. It is impossible to surrender to the Divine as long as we are egoistic. You need a very, very deep connection with God, then you can surrender; otherwise you will keep up your individual attitudes and, inevitably, you will do everything you can to sustain them. In fact, you will prefer to strengthen them more and more. The ability to give yourself to the Divine only comes when you have a great, great love for God—a nonhuman love. Only then can you give your ego to the Divine."

***In the West, women are trying to reintegrate our divine potential, which will nourish our ability to accept what is, to face the challenges we are going through, to find faith in life and in ourselves.***

"You cannot surrender yourself to abstract ideas like this," Mataji interrupts. "What are you surrendering anyway? Your money, your health, your appearance, your body?"

"Ego attachment!" I reply emphatically.

"Ah, that's it! But to what do you surrender?" She laughs with gusto. "You can only surrender to divine power! Without that, and without love for divinity, you cannot know what it means to surrender to God."

"I cannot say that I want to surrender to life?" I ask her.

"What is life?" she asks in return.

"Life is the Divine; it is divine power."

"Life is not only divine manifestation. What you call life is not real," Mataji laughs again, still amused.

She is right; it is the maya, or illusion, we spoke about earlier.

"You are surrendering to something unreal—how will that work?" she asks. "It does not work that way. We can only rely on something far, far, far superior to us, which at the same time is so intimate, so wonderful, and so beautiful—otherwise you are just playing with words; it means nothing."

Mataji's incontrovertible clarity on the one hand disorients my thinking and, on the other, reorients my internal compass. I am suddenly questioning the New Age attitude of "trusting the universe" and "going with the flow" so prevalent in Western spiritual communities. This now feels like a naive and limiting approach to relating to the Divine. Compared with direct knowledge of and surrender to the Divine, it seems ungrounded and weak. I can't yet fully grasp what she's saying, but I feel hope, and sometimes hope is worth a great deal. Even if that hope doesn't come from a deep inner matrix or doesn't reach my cells, it is like relying on external support. Like a balloon can save a child from sadness, hope can save an adult from despair. After all, what does one do if one does not yet have direct experience of the Divine? Hope to stumble into it by grace. By giving it attention and care, we can grow faith in the unknown.

***On the spiritual path, how important is mutual support between women?***

"You may have married the best man in the world and have all the beautiful children you want, but it will always be important to cultivate female friendships," Mataji maintains. "This is why we also have many festivals here in India where women gather. In the past, when women got married, they would leave their family home and cry at the idea of never seeing their loved ones again. Only on certain occasions were they allowed to return, so it was very important for them to have female friends with whom they could have fun and get through difficult times and who could support them. Only a woman can know a woman's heart. Men cannot really know what a woman is truly about!"

I agree wholeheartedly, yet this is precisely the wonderful mystery—that the gap between men and women (or the masculine and feminine) can also allow for a spark to ignite and for the unknown to sneak in. And this is also why women know how to support each other in truly creative and spontaneous ways. When doing spiritual group work, this capacity immediately emerges. It is the emotional intelligence of the heart that, in a group of women, is often amplified so much that it proves capable of working true miracles, such as transforming hard emotions into a river of tears or feeling completely at ease to open up and be vulnerable in a group of people we don't actually know.

Women often have a range of complexes about their appearance. We are rarely happy with how we look and are almost always racing toward the best version of ourselves. I ask Mataji, whose inner beauty shines so brightly, about how these superficial efforts relate to our spiritual quest and our attempts to understand who we really are and who we are not.

"Today, there is so much stress on physical appearance," she says. "So many beauty products, clothes, this and that . . . but no matter what you do to make yourself beautiful outwardly, true beauty will not just emerge from that. Outer beauty only lasts a few years; it does not last forever. Instead, inner beauty, which depends on kindness, compassion, the desire to help others, and maternal instincts—these are the qualities that women have and that you can cultivate. These constitute the true beauty of a woman.

"Some women, even of a certain old age, have a very attractive aura of love around them because of their inner beauty. When girls are young, of course, it's OK for them to make themselves pretty and all; it's not a problem. Don't go around with messy hair and wrinkled clothes—after all you are a goddess! But not all deities are beautiful externally. Think of Kali, Durga, Chandi—we have so many goddesses who are not beautiful in appearance but are very forceful. Women should try to cultivate, above all, the inner feminine qualities that are unique to them. Then beauty will automatically come out."

Mataji also offered an image that really landed with me: If you want to see a plant flourish, water the roots, not the branches. If you want to experience your flowering as a woman, but you keep watering only the branches, then you will never grow into your potential. If, on the other hand, you water the roots, if you search for who you are deep down, if you connect to yourself at that fundamental level and recover your connection to the Divine that characterizes and nourishes your being, then your true beauty will blossom accordingly and naturally. Attention should therefore go to the heart. We should tend to the heart as the most important aspect of our inner world. Attend it, welcome it, love it. Bring the sun into your inner world and light the path.

Outer beauty flows from the heart. When the heart is oiled, the best of who we are is expressed in all its fragrances, even our appearance. It's just like when we are in love, and we become more beautiful than usual, such that everyone around us seems to notice it. Our skin glows, our eyes sparkle, and a whole series of systemic operations come into action so that we emit a radiance.

Mataji confirms that we can also support ourselves by taking care of ourselves on the outside, keeping fit and making ourselves beautiful. The important thing is that the heart is showered with attention and that the primary inner work that needs to be done does not take second, third, or fourth place. Otherwise, we will inevitably grow up crooked, with a distorted view of ourselves that will eventually imprison us. Only the truth can free us. Sometimes we lose sight of the absolute priority of our inner well-being and believe that we will achieve it when we are as beautiful as we want to be. This becomes an absurd vicious circle. If we strive too hard, eager and anxious to be seen and appreciated, then the effort will sully our essence, which feels offended and forgotten. If, on the other hand, we love ourselves and know how to smile with gentleness at the changes that our body goes through, then we will transmit the grace and immense freedom of inhabiting an unjudged body—the absolute beauty of knowing how to live in balance with what is.

The idea that "your body is a temple" is a common image in yogic traditions, but it is often used as a reminder to focus on the superficial rather than the meaningful aspects of our physical existence. We would do well to keep the body healthy, alive, and regal because we value the spirit that dwells within the temple of the body and because we can experience union with the Divine through this body. I want this body to be clean and cared for, yet I do not want to become a slave to its image or to its form. The point is not to be preoccupied with the architecture of the temple but to serve the spirit through the life that we create space for within the temple of our body.

I am learning to respect my body and honor it, but a nagging point keeps surfacing: How do I open to the Divine? Sometimes the temple is inhabited and sometimes it feels empty.

***How do we fully and practically integrate with the Divine?***

"The supreme Divine is beyond duality," Mataji answers. "Female and male are the same. We all live in this dimension of time and space and causality because that is how the mind works. It is what we have been taught. But the Divine is in everything—in every creature, in every star, in every flower. So how can you talk about reconciliation? *Aham asmi*—'I am the Divine,' 'I am Brahman.' Not only can women and men say this, but also any dog or cat. Only the human being, however, is able to understand and experience this. You are intellectually playing with words. You are saying, 'I am a woman, I am a woman.' Yes, you are a woman, yet you do not need to say it! You are the Divine! I do not need to tell you again. You are. You are everything. I am.

"The Divine does not differentiate in any way. Everything is That, and That is all. Since That is, everything is. Since That is conscious, everything is conscious. All life is One. There is no two. Everything is an emanation of that One. We are already complete, but we are ignorant, and so we perceive continuous differentiation and feel ourselves to be just a part of the whole that is separate from the rest. We ignore who we are. This is the original sin in Hinduism. When that knowledge finally arises, we realize the unity of life. Life is a whole; it is not divided into compartments. PURNAMADAH PURNAMIDAM, meaning 'That is full, this is also full.' From the full when you take away something, what remains? Fullness. Because you can never take away from that which is full. Subtraction is not possible in this realm beyond logic. It is there, and it will always be full. It cannot be cut into pieces. It is One. In differentiation it can manifest itself, just as electricity can manifest itself in various forms: in the fan, in the light, in the refrigerator, in the oven . . . but the power is One. It is not two."

Clearly the electricity is flowing through Mataji at this moment! As it strikes, it takes away every mental quibble of mine. I ask her, as a final question, to recommend a female deity to whom we can turn for guidance or protection.

"Durga!" she exclaims. "She is the eternal feminine. She has no consort. She does not depend on anyone for her power. She is said to have been created by male deities, using the best of their powers, to kill Mahishasura, a demon. She was generated by fire and is the very epitome of what it means to be a woman.

"But all female deities are powerful, and each has different characteristics and her own department. For good auspices, we pray to Lakshmi. For art, science, and wisdom, we pray to Saraswati. In ancient times, men—before going into battle—prayed to Durga, because she is the one who wins wars. Finally, in the Vedas, the goddess of the earth is praised as Prithvi. She is our first mother.

"From the earth we are born, and to the earth we will return when we die. It has always been part of our tradition to touch the earth, Prithvi, our first mother, as soon as we get out of bed in the morning and to ask for her forgiveness for stepping on her during the day.

Our children have been taught from an early age to revere her great stability and inexhaustible fertility. Our veneration for our rivers and mountains also stems from this. Our rivers are known as goddesses, for the ancients knew them to be the arteries of the country—our very lifeblood—pumping their inexhaustible fund of life-giving waters from the mountains to the sea."

I breathe a sigh of relief and acknowledgment as the interview comes to a close. Mataji recites a beautiful prayer that ends with a very sweet OM SHANTI SHANTI HARI OM and adds "Again, Shanti, or Peace, is the name of a woman. And on that note, let us close."

Mataji's laughter tickles my brain, teasing my limited mind. She recommends her book *The Hindu Way of Life*, and while I question adding another book to the pile that I am traveling with, of course I take it. While it feels increasingly absurd to travel around India like a wandering library, I would rather abandon some clothes for more knowledge. Perhaps I will end up like Mataji, with just a simple one-colored dress.

This conversation with Mataji was challenging. I need to immerse myself in the Ganges, the river that is a Divine Mother. I feel I have concepts to let go of, and I hope the current carries them away.

The golden light of the sunset is taking its final bath of the day. Standing there, in the middle of such beauty, I realize that a woman finds her strength at the expense of no one and without fighting. We are perfectly in our place already, and we can always find the creative strength of the whole universe inside us and become immersed in it. With the power of water, we can regain the full extent of our reservoir of truth. As I stand absorbed in the moment, the icy current presses me to bear all my weight on the soles of my feet, balancing on the slippery stones.

It's as if everything is already within us, but we need a key to see it. A simple key—yet the mind cannot rest in that simplicity. It complicates it. It invents a path to follow. It creates obstacles to overcome. It creates confusion and misunderstandings of every kind. It forges side paths and even sows doubts about what we are truly venerating. In essence, the mind makes the Divine—always accessible—seem inaccessible. Knocking might be enough.

In knowing the Divine, there is no doubt that it is the end of all these mental parodies. And so, I find myself wanting to remain silent, to place no trust or hope in the mind or its movements. As Antonella Lumini said, silence is truly the place where God arises. And I recall Jetsunma Tenzin Palmo's advice to befriend this restless monkey mind rather than fight it, but to keep a certain distance. These different words of wisdom converge into a single intention.

And what does it mean that all women are goddesses, daughters of the Divine Mother? Even this, only each of us within ourselves can truly know. These things must be known from within. One must meet Her at the end of oneself—only to discover that She has been there from the beginning. The Divine Mother is in the mirror, just beyond the veil.

12

# Flush with Brilliant Aliveness

## RABBI JULIA WATTS BELSER

When we bring deep care and interest to a subject, when we offer it our regard—whether it's another human being or a bird sitting on the wire outside our house—anything can open us up to the infinite ocean.

—RABBI JULIA WATTS BELSER

Reading Julia Watts Belser's book *Loving Our Own Bones*, I was stunned from the first page to the last. I felt healed by her marvelous revisitation of the Torah through the lens of disability, and, for the first time, I saw God on wheels. It had been a long time since I last read a book that made me stop in sheer wonder—the kind of wonder that compels you to pause, reread aloud, and savor the perfect sentences that act as true portals to a precious dimension of being. In every page, you can sense her questioning and waiting for an answer that feels right—it's the record of an excavation through years, bones, and flesh.

Julia Watts Belser is a scholar, writer, and rabbi whose work explores the intersection of disability, Jewish theology, gender, and environmental justice. She invites us to rethink accessibility—not just as a physical or social issue but as a sacred practice. Talking with Julia was an even more fascinating experience than reading her book. She is one of those rare people who speaks the way she writes.

***Can you tell me how your spiritual journey began?***

"Spiritual life has always been core to my lived experience," Julia replies. "As I look back on my childhood, I can see how deeply a sense of awe and wonder gave shape to my life. A sense of being in the presence of the sacred has always run like a bright thread though my days. It feels to me that *presence* is the best way of describing it. Sometimes I use the word *God*, but that word comes with a lot of assumptions I don't mean. I'm speaking about the presence that runs through all of life: the shimmer, the aliveness that makes the birds want to sing and draws the flowers to grow. Not just the gorgeous flowers, the ones we cultivate, but also the dandelions that push their way up through cracks in the concrete—that force, that sense of vitality, beauty, fierceness, and persistent deliberate hope. That's what I mean when I think of the sacred. That's what I mean when I think of God. That's the center of my life and work. I hope to always be turning toward that presence: looking for it, listening for it, tasting it, loving it, reflecting it in the world, and making more of it.

"The sacred is bigger and deeper than any particular religious tradition. When I was ordained as a rabbi, it was the reflection of a commitment to steward and honor sacred presence and to bring it into relationship with Jewish tradition. But this work was alive in me before I became a rabbi. It feels important to name that this presence, this life force, this aliveness that we might call God—it is not owned by anyone. It is something that we serve and honor and try to bring forth into the world. It's alive in all our traditions, in their best moments. It's alive in all of us, or it could be."

***Most of us probably experienced something similar during childhood—that sense of an all-pervading magic that later in life we recognize as life's sacredness. However, we often lose touch with that spark as we grow up and eventually forget it altogether. How did you keep that spark alive in yourself?***

"Even as a child, I felt aware that this presence was vital and precious," Julia says. "I didn't want to lose it. I also felt that it was hungry for my attention, for all our attention. To give attention to the sacred is a way of helping it grow. I cultivated a kind of holy stubbornness: Why should I give it up? Why should I let it go? This sense that the world is flush with brilliant aliveness—why should we shrug it off as an artifact of childhood? It deserves to be a part of our ways of being in the world.

"I've always felt a bit out of step with other people. While that feeling of difference was sometimes painful, it was also part of how I kept the sacred alive in my life. There was so much I didn't understand about the social dynamics of being a teenager: dating and makeup and all that. I didn't understand it. I didn't want to understand it, so I turned my attention elsewhere. I allowed myself to cultivate a loving, sensuous relationship with earth and stones and birds and trees. I gave my attention and my care to the wild luminous presence. And I let myself fall in love with words, with story, with this vibrant inner life.

"I don't want to romanticize loneliness. Growing up, there were moments when my own disability experience, queer experience, and gendered experience left me feeling out of place. But I think one of the beautiful things to come from that loneliness was the decision to turn ever more deeply toward this sense of the sacred. It remained alive in my life in part because I gave it—and continue to give it—time, attention, and regard."

***This makes me reflect on how attention has the potential to become love. Of course, not every time we pay attention to something are we in a state of openness and loving receptivity. But attention seems to be that first step we take toward the world, the intention to be fully present with anything, any situation, or any person. In your experience, how do love and attention come together in spiritual practice?***

"The relationship between love and attention is a vibrant part of my own spiritual practice," Julia asserts. "One thing that disability has taught me is to have deep regard for small things and small pleasures. Before the pandemic, I had the immense privilege of traveling quite widely. But because I'm at risk of significant complications from COVID, my world has now become quite small. I feel it very intimately: The way that disabled people and others who are at higher risk of harm have been abandoned by our society and shut out of public spaces because of the way that risk has been privatized. Some days it hollows out my heart: the political betrayal, the crushing disregard of a world that's just moved on.

"But even here, even now, there are possibilities for spiritual practice. These past years have been an extraordinary opportunity to deepen my own practice of attention, to give deep and close regard to the intimate space of my own backyard. It is a small space: a little garden that I tend with love, a patch of grass, a thicket of brush and bushes, a few tall sentinel trees. It is a home I share with crows and cardinals, with song sparrows and squirrels, with rabbits and deer, and a fox who raises her kits under the back deck. It is a small space, and it is a vast universe. There is a Jewish teaching that says that to destroy a single life is to destroy an entire world. That insight feels very potent to me. When we bring deep care and interest to a subject, when we offer it our regard—whether it's another human being or a bird sitting on the wire outside our house—anything can open us up to the infinite ocean."

And yet, at times, details seem so elusive, absorbed as we are by the big picture. Perhaps it is precisely in those moments that we should pause, even for an instant, and make the effort to grasp the beauty of a single tiny detail. Even just a glimpse of it can soften the overall tension of an entire course of action, running after an outcome. In doing so, we might discover the ease that always resides beyond time.

***The dimension you speak of seems to exist outside of time itself and be related to our capacity of vision, which at times shrinks and at other times expands and becomes more inclusive.***

"The Jewish practice of Shabbat has really shaped my thinking about time," Julia says thoughtfully, "and it's given me tools to cultivate the spaciousness you're talking about. The traditional understanding of Shabbat is that you set aside twenty-five hours each week to savor the world as it is. From eighteen minutes before sundown on Friday night until the first three stars come out on Saturday, Shabbat gives us this long expanse of sweet time that is not to be spent doing labor. Jews keep Shabbat in many ways; there's tremendous variation in how people practice. For me, it's about not doing work, not carrying money, not checking my emails, not thinking about my job, and not investing in the act of creative making. All those limits open up a spaciousness, a way of being present with the world as it is.

"Of course, this is a tremendously difficult practice, if one takes it seriously. It's not just a matter of not working; it's a call to not even think about work. Teaching myself to keep that practice has forced me to recognize how often my work life colonizes my inner being. But week after week, I carve out the spaciousness to just actually be with myself, my loved ones, the earth, my bed—to let myself sink into rest and into a certain kind of stillness. It has become the cornerstone of my practice: to train my mind to come back to that expansive, spacious presence, to hone the practice and the skill of not always allowing my mind to be owned by work."

***This "stepping back" sounds like the same attitude we have when sitting in meditation. The mind has this inherent habit of compulsively engaging, and it makes us believe that we can't stop. If we do manage to stop, we start feeling guilty. Do you find this becomes a practice also of not believing everything we think and slowly releasing all our mental constructs?***

"Disability has spurred me to think much more clearly about limits, to come to grips with the fact that rest is not a luxury," says Julia. "It's helped me understand something about the importance of releasing certain expectations. In some ways, for example, my own Shabbat practice is deeply tuned to Jewish tradition. But in other respects, it's quite unconventional. In many Jewish communities, the most central part of Shabbat is Friday night dinner. It's a very social celebration: Family and friends and guests come together to eat and talk and laugh and sing. But by the time my body and mind have made it to the end of the week, I'm often in a place of deep weariness. The thought of having people over for an elaborate meal on Friday night feels utterly impossible. Part of that is disability; part of that is just my own nature. I'm a deeply quiet person. My soul is fed by stillness. Shabbat for me is sinking into that stillness, letting the luminous darkness and the flickering candles bathe my heart in holy quiet.

"This willingness to both honor the deep resources of my own tradition and to reshape them feels emblematic of what I bring as a feminist, as a queer, and as a disabled spiritual teacher. I have profound respect and appreciation for the wisdom of my tradition. Yet at the same time, I don't trust the normative voice of my tradition to know the truth of my own experience or to speak adequately to my own needs. There's a loyalty and a dissidence that go hand in hand in my work. I want to be taught by the best of my tradition. I want to take it very seriously and allow it to challenge some of my presumptions and assumptions. I think it matters that we allow ourselves to be schooled by sources of wisdom that are deeper and wider than our own lives. Yet I also ground myself in a fierce commitment to bring my own knowledge and my own dissident fire to Jewish tradition, to talk back to its authoritative voice and say, 'Actually, you don't know the truth of my life.' There are so many ways in which my lived experience as a woman, as a queer person, as a disabled person is so profoundly disregarded by my tradition. My work is to keep both positions close, to dance with them, to figure out when to say yes and when to say no."

I can relate to Julia's search for balance, which is also a constant endeavor for me in this sacred work on women's spirituality. It is not about creating something entirely new but about preserving the beauty and power of traditions without being bound by certain dogmas or dictates that no longer resonate with our present reality. I believe great discernment is needed to understand how far critical thinking can serve the spiritual path, to what extent we should invite innovation in certain aspects, and when, instead, we must surrender—letting go of perspectives we might be too attached to. It truly is a delicate dance. How can we honor and remain faithful to spiritual traditions that hold so much wisdom, while also "breaking" them or opening their shell where they are rigid around dogmas and beliefs that are not aligned with an integrated spirituality?

"When I was in rabbinical school," Julia continues, "I realized how important it was to crack open the way we think about canon. What's sacred? My tradition is steeped in sacred words: We immerse ourselves not just in the text of the Torah but also the centuries of commentary and midrash that have developed to expand and deepen the text. The tradition is words upon words layered upon more words. Almost all those words have been men's words.

"For me, the answer can't simply be to add another layer of commentary on top of existing commentary. Sometimes the very fabric and framework of tradition feels like too tight a box. There's a risk here for minoritized communities: We get lured into the project of responding to the wrong questions. All our energy gets drawn into responding to the way someone else has imagined our own lives. I want us to crack open fresh spaces for imagining differently. There's so much of the Torah that we need. We need sacred stories told unapologetically from a feminist and queer and disability perspective, from a trans perspective, from a woman of color perspective. The work that disability communities are doing today to reimagine what care looks like, to refuse stigma and shame, to stay alive in a world that is so often hostile to our own existence—that's sacred work. That's work and wisdom that deserves to be recognized as part of our lineage of sacred sources. One of my core commitments as a rabbi is a commitment to bring disability wisdom back to my own tradition. The Torah needs this wisdom. It needs us. It's not just a matter of learning from the sacred text. I believe we also have an obligation to bring what we know of the sacred into the fabric of our own traditions."

***And this is what you have done in your latest book,* Loving Our Own Bones, *where you revisited the Torah through the lens of disability, offering an interpretation that is both profoundly original and no less authentic in its engagement with the sacred text. How has disability shaped and supported your research?***

"Disability is a dissident way of being in the world," Julia tells me. "People often imagine disability as a kind of diminishment or lack. But I find it more fruitful to recognize disability as a form of generative difference: a different way of being, sensing, knowing, and moving through this world. Take one example: We live in a world that assumes everyone should pay attention in the same way. But when we center on disability, it allows us to recognize that there are a thousand different ways of knowing. Our ways of thinking and our ways of feeling are incredibly diverse. Spiritual life isn't a one-size-fits-all enterprise. Thinking politically about disability gives us powerful tools for critiquing stigma and normativity, for pushing back on the assumption that everyone's body-mind works in the same way. Every disabled person I know has stories about the cost of living in a world that doesn't want us or that didn't plan for us. We get shut out. We get pushed aside. We get left behind.

"Taking disability seriously asks us to push back on the assumption that all bodies and minds should be the same. The difference of our bodies and minds is generative and worth honoring in the world, even when it's complicated. Especially when it's complicated. Even when it's an experience marked by pain and loss and real complexity. It matters to take difference seriously, to recognize it as something that is good for our world and good for God."

***Why is there so much hesitation in embracing diversity?***

"That's the question, isn't it?" Julia asks in return. "It feels like it would take a lifetime to unravel the intricacies of ableism and disability disdain. So let me address one strand: the way I came to recognize disability as something worth embracing. I use the term *embrace* deliberately. I find myself interested in the practice of turning more generously toward disability—even when it's challenging, even when it's difficult. I'm curious about the possibilities it might offer, about the insights it might allow to unfold.

"Take just one example: Disability has brought me into intimate understanding of the ways in which our mind, body, and bones are always in flux. The only constant for bodies is that they change. This is one of the ways I think disability wisdom can be a potent resource for all of us, especially for people who don't yet know disability intimately. I think it can offer us a gentler way of being present with our own bodies and minds. Many of us speak in quite a hostile way toward our bodies, especially when our bodies are letting us down. I berate my hips when they tighten; I get angry with my knees when they ache. When we experience forgetfulness, anxiety, brain fog, depression, or grief, we often direct the same kind of cruelty toward our own minds. But over the years, I've been teaching myself a different kind of practice. Instead of maligning my own bones, I reach out a hand to cradle the place that hurts. I offer myself soft words, as though I were speaking to a friend. I want to build a practice of turning toward ourselves with tenderness. I believe we can teach ourselves to offer love and kindness toward our own bodies and minds."

These words touch me deeply because I know exactly what it means to move from cursing physical pain to surrendering to it and almost even embracing it. Sometimes, we fail to take care of the parts of ourselves that are struggling. Our arms are not long enough to reach us as we fall into the shadow, and our patience is not refined enough to gently bear the weight of some inner cracks when we get disappointed. We lose heart too soon in this inner landscape, where anything can happen—and does. We lack the wisdom to sit with everything as if it were simply part of the scenery. Our inner volcanoes turn us to dust, our tides overwhelm us, and to avoid it all, we cling to clichés of thought, to the collective anchors that have been expressed over time as lifesaving remedies. We shut ourselves off from what is different to preserve those anchors, that sense of what is "normal." True salvation lies in looking at our existential condition with clarity, generous attention, and courage—understanding that it is made up of a staggering diversity. Accepting this sense of bewilderment and holding it within us as a treasure might eventually allow us to embrace even the most distant parts of ourselves—the ones that keep their distance and remain hidden as long as we remain so cautious and narrow-minded.

***I really loved the idea of a God in a wheelchair in your book. It's something I had never thought of before, but as soon as I read it, it felt obvious—of course, since God is everything. How did this idea of God in a wheelchair arise in you?***

"One of the most profound spiritual reorientations in my life was the recognition that God is not distant from disability," Julia answers.

"God knows disability from the inside. As a person who uses a wheelchair, I've found it quite transformative to turn toward a God on wheels, to turn toward a God who knows the exquisite pleasures of a life lived on wheels, a God who knows the pleasure of a long, gentle downhill grade, a God who knows the beauty of a spin.

"I became a wheelchair user after a long period where walking was intensely painful. Getting my own wheels felt like liberation. It was freedom. It was joy. But it also brought me face-to-face with all the ways this world isn't built for people like me. That's another spiritual truth I hold: If God knows life on wheels, God knows also how it feels to be shut out. God knows the frustration of the locked lift and the building without an elevator. God knows all the endless ways in which our human-made systems and structures create barriers to entry, over and over again.

"Spiritual seekers often talk about wanting to get close to God, but I find it quite evocative to think about God as the one who gets shut out of our hearts. It puts a new spin on the question, How do we crack open space for divine presence? Can we shift our inner architecture? Can we soften the barriers we've made? How do we open the door so that sacredness, awe, wonder, beauty, and wholeness can flow into and through us without getting clogged up in all our assumptions and all our denials?

"There's a strand of Jewish mystical wisdom that teaches that there's nothing in this world that is not God. It's all infinite divine presence. Of course, it's difficult to access that in everyday moments. But I think of my childhood self lying down upon the ground and feeling her own body and bones dissolve into the earth, knowing herself utterly inseparable from holy presence. I want to ease away all the impediments to that knowing. I want that for myself, and I want that for us all."

I feel a deep resonance with Julia's words, to the point that they feel like my own thoughts, only better expressed. Perhaps this is the only true *fil rouge*—literally, "red thread" but figuratively, common thread or central theme—running through all spiritual traditions: God is a constant presence and awareness is always available, but we flee and get distracted and find excuses to miss the only appointment we are here for. The Divine awaits us, ready to receive and embrace us, but are we ready to surrender and offer ourselves? Or are we stuck, lost in our inner architecture and unable to find the door? Maybe we are so many and so different because we can somehow guide each other back home, to the oneness we are and deeply belong to. By including each other's differences, we are moving forward toward that.

***Do you think we are here to accompany each other to the realization that we are already home?***

"Yes, I think that's true," Julia agrees. "But I also want to lift up the obligation to transform not just our patterns of thought but also the material world in which we live. This is the core obligation that grounds my spiritual life: to work for a world where everyone is safe from harm. A world where everyone has food and shelter. A world where everyone has access to meaningful, dignified health care. A world where there is no war. A world where all living beings can flourish and thrive.

"My root conviction is we must not dichotomize these things. My commitment to material care and nurture and justice is the very lifeblood of that feeling of being cradled by the ground. I want us to commit to the long, slow work that makes it possible for people to have the spaciousness and well-being to sink into that sweetness, to know themselves absolutely and utterly loved. Of course, people can find the sacred anywhere. The door is always open, even in the most constrained circumstances. But I believe we have an obligation to make the circumstances as easeful as possible. We owe that to each other.

"There's a Jewish tradition from the Talmud that says, *Im ein kemach, ein Torah*, meaning that if there's no flour, if there's no bread, there's no Torah. When we are committed to spiritual work, we are also committed to the work of feeding people, of peacemaking, of creating the tangible conditions that make it possible for us all to live."

And so, here we are in our temple of bone, flesh, and blood. The heart is always knocking on the temple doors—from the inside. It wants to open them, to offer access to the Divine. Every moment is deeply rooted in this longing for unconditional openness.

The sacred must be nourished.

As Julia Watts Belser so poignantly writes, "I also felt that it was hungry for my attention, for all of our attention." There is a hunger in the sacred—not for things, not for answers, but for presence. For devotion. For the simple act of turning toward it with care.

A woman's body carries within it an ancient memory—the innate, embodied knowing of how to nourish. It responds, almost effortlessly, to the call of life needing to be sustained. This is not learned; it is remembered. It is the root of all beginnings. Just as a mother offers herself wholly—body, time, and spirit—to feed her child, so too can we offer ourselves, in full presence, to feed the sacred.

It is not the mind alone that prays. Prayer rises from the ground of the body, when it sinks into presence. The mind does not lead at all—it listens. It quiets, softens, and makes space. And in that spaciousness, something sacred begins to bloom.

Attention becomes a form of devotion. It is how the sacred grows. "To give attention to the sacred is a way of helping it grow," Julia said. It's not a grand gesture. It's the daily turning, the quiet noticing, the gentle returning. Again and again. We tend to it as we would a child: We follow it, listen for it, and call it by name. We give ourselves to it—daily, gently, with devotion—so we do not lose the thread. "I cultivated a kind of holy stubbornness," Julia stated. Why should we ever lose that thread of the sacred, the one that has run through our lives since the moment we were born? Why should we resist the invitation to slip into its current, to rest in its mystery?

Let the act of merging with nature—of knowing ourselves as part of a vast, enchanted whole—not be a gift reserved for the very young.

Let the power to nourish life not be held by women alone.

Let the sacred belong to all.

And may it always be an honor to feed it.

# EMERGENCE

Since the moment the dam of my personal Great Flood let go, I have encountered an immeasurable amount of grace. Despite the gifts of wisdom and insight I have received, I haven't been spared the experience of a considerable amount of darkness, misery, and shame. These radiant encounters have held me, shaped me, and, as all good teachings do, illuminated the places I still couldn't see. I have been working tirelessly to bring forth women's wisdom without realizing I was doing it the old way—pushing through like a mule, neglecting myself in the name of a higher goal. I had no idea how strongly that conditioning still lived in me, but by being exposed to so much kindness, love, and presence, I have seen how harsh and demanding I've been with myself. The thread running through all my conversations with these women is this: You don't go anywhere if you don't embrace yourself first.

Like many women, I had been trained to achieve, to keep going and not stop to take time for myself or to check how I am doing. And so I applied that same approach to my spiritual path—disavowing parts of my life and myself, meditating and practicing like a soldier determined to escape samsara. But then the sacred feminine broke through and offered me a new life. I'm only just beginning to walk this new way of being—where feeling leads, where there is more space, and where meeting oneself is a continuous, beautiful unfolding. I offer you an invitation to walk with me.

How do we make this transition? Meditation and the practice of awareness help because we become more able to *see*. As we get to know who we are as a person, examining our dynamics closely, this helps us detach from them. For me, when I began this project, I had no idea how much fear was locked up in me. By engaging with the world in this way, coming out of my shell, those fears came out too. *What if I don't have the skills for this? What if I screw it up? Am I worthy of such an endeavor? Am I worthy of the love that could come in my life if I say 'Yes' to the mission of my heart?* We must cultivate the qualities we need to hold ourselves steady within this transformation—compassion, loving-kindness, clarity, gentle persistence, trust, and patience. Thanks to these, we can see when unskillful doubts rooted in false beliefs arise and let them go. We can reassure ourselves by addressing these doubts in a compassionate and loving way: *Thank you for your concern. I'm doing the best I can with the resources I have right now. It might not be perfect or ideal, but it is what I can do for now. And I'm going to keep going.*

Like a snake shedding its skin, I now see the old armor of conditioning that elevated masculine wisdom and devalued feminine wisdom beginning to dry upon my surface. I glimpse it every time I notice a limiting pattern and choose, instead, the path of softness and care. And I know that one day that old skin will fall away on its own, dropping gently into a field somewhere—so gently, perhaps, I won't even notice I've left it behind. This is the initiation of the divine feminine that, for me, comes through the presence and teachings of the women I've had the good fortune to encounter.

And then comes the discovery of the heart, seen in a different light. When I am alone with myself, is there love? When I make tea, fold a blanket, or speak to my own heart is there care in how I inhabit my own space when no one is around? How do I hold my heart in moments of pain and struggle? Do I know how to acknowledge difficult emotions without being swept away by them? Do I let my heart breathe with the sky?

Through these conversations, I began to notice the absence of love for myself, realizing there had never been the space or the intention to let it grow. Softening has become one of my greatest lessons—and it remains a work in progress. The most tender question I now carry close to my heart is this: Can I be gentle with myself? Often, kindness toward oneself is simply about choosing not to be harsh, not to criticize, not to judge. It's allowing ourselves to be messy, to not have it all figured out, to rest in not knowing, and to find peace even in the presence of our deepest blind spots.

From this one question flow many others that are similar and that now travel with me: Can I be assertive with kindness? Can I be fiercely compassionate? Can I be steady with lightness? Can I be strong in a soft way? Can I accept that there is a bird full of love in my chest that has been caged for most of my life by false beliefs? Can I feel its vulnerability and choose every day to be soft, to acknowledge it? Can I let love be free to express itself in whatever way it wants to manifest?

Devoting myself to women of wisdom—their voices, their presence, their messages—reminds me, again and again, that there is nothing more to do but welcome the wisdom of tenderness into everyday life. Sometimes, attention softens, and light pools in the corners of the room. The house becomes a sanctuary. The breath becomes a blessing. In those moments, I sense the teachers of the heart are here, each one whispering how to tend a different garden of this wild, beautiful life. And it flows effortlessly.

Other times, it's harder or even impossible to tune in. The mind becomes heavy, caught up with familiar fears, new insecurities, and obscurities not yet attended. It seeks distractions. Yet, by staying curious, by remaining open to this process, I've found that my capacity for vision and kindness grows. Intention is the most powerful force at play here; the rest is about letting go.

Sometimes, we don't realize there's another way of being, of doing things. We carry on living as our parents did, or as we have seen others do. This is why encountering new perspectives and role models can be lifesaving. I deeply believe in the healing power that comes from bringing women of wisdom into the light and in allowing ourselves to be changed by the feminine path. To open the door if it has been closed. To let that healing power flow in its full capacity, if it already lives within us.

I didn't know I had this power within me: to choose to tremble with love instead of stiffening with fear, to survive the temptation to close the doors when times get tough. To choose to say, "Times are hard, the heart is wounded, the soul weeps," and still choose to say: "Yes, we carry ancient pains within us, but we don't need to shut down—we can stay open. More love can be planted here. We can protect the heart with loving-kindness instead of using the walls of fear. We can go through the change; we can be in it down to the bone. There is no need to hold back. It's worth it—to give ourselves fully."

The scope of this inquiry has far exceeded my expectations—there is no single thread to follow. The spiritual life of women opens a field that is inherently multidimensional. One dimension concerns the empowerment of women, revealing that what has long been called the "weaker sex" is, in truth, the strong-soft sex. Women's particular strength flourishes only with the right cultural and social ecosystem—one that is currently lacking in our world, and whose lack has had dire consequences. It is in everyone's best interest for women to step into their full power: strong in themselves and supported by the world around them.

Women must rise—and are rising—but how? This brings us to another dimension: the dynamic interplay between feminine and masculine energies. When women assert themselves by mirroring masculine negative models, nothing is truly gained. What is needed is a reclamation of the feminine force—its vitality, its intelligence—and a reimagining of how to embody it in the contemporary paradigms of work, creativity, and expression. At this moment, women need virtuous role models—whole, luminous, and deeply feminine in the truest sense of the word. The richness of that word—*feminine*—must be rediscovered because women everywhere are trembling on the verge of a new way, ready to manifest it.

But the journey doesn't end there. The feminine is not merely a gendered attribute; it is a cosmic polarity. Regardless of how we identify, we are called to reconnect with the sacred feminine. Together, we can leap beyond gender and see the feminine and masculine as complementary polarities of being, each with its light and its shadow. For too long, the world has been dominated by the shadow of the masculine: violence, aggressive assertion, immediate gratification, and the rigid structures (the ones we call normal) that are causing tremendous damage to the planet. With new eyes, we can begin to see differently and shift these patterns.

This sacred feminine is a turning toward the cosmos with wonder—a visionary gaze that pierces the surface of matter to glimpse what lies beyond. It is the unseen thread binding spirit and substance in the subtlest, most ineffable way. To uplift the invisible becomes an act of healing—a refinement of the inner senses, an awakening of our capacity to truly listen. In this listening, a portal to the Divine quietly opens, and we begin to tune ourselves to reality with compassion, care, and purpose. There, within that resonance, we encounter the unity within ourselves and between us and connect with the earth with respect and gratitude.

This feminine power concerns us all. Many men are doing incredible work to find balance within themselves, allowing their feminine side to emerge and letting emotions flow while maintaining their core. It's not easy, and I deeply appreciate the effort that men are making to stand beside us in new ways. We shall guide each other.

The Divine does not have a gender—only a fool would think so—but conceiving of it as a Divine Mother or as a womb helps us approach its essence. It is the pure potentiality of form, whose nature is clarity and luminosity, whose expression is compassion. Everything arises from it and is inseparable from it. Even when we are exhausted and lost, we remain in the embrace of the Divine Mother, where we can rest and regain clarity. To be present and recognize the pregnant nature of light is an act of awareness that unites formless space and infinite empty forms. I know this sounds abstract, but it is not. It is what we do when we become aware of our own thoughts and then of the awareness itself. It is like giving ourselves an inner kiss, returning to our true home.

This is not about preferring the feminine to the masculine or women to men. It is not about saying that the masculine approach that we have been exposed to so far in most religions is wrong. It is not wrong! It works. For some people, it is the perfect path. For others, it doesn't resonate anymore. So here we are making space for something different. We all have the opportunity to rest deeply in our true nature, in the womb of the Great Mother, in the Divine, in the light of awareness. And we can get there through gentle ways, by becoming aware of the secret dream of union within.

From the beginning, this journey has been a necessary wandering. Initially, I thought it was about recovering the feminine universe, but now I see it leads to the wholeness that exists beyond the dance of opposites—toward the exquisite fullness and sacredness of the union that already resides within us. It leads to embracing and allowing and guiding toward it everything that stands within it. The iceberg I initially crashed into has melted into an ocean that belongs to everyone and to no one—waters that are identical in each of us.

We long to return to the source of life, to the foot of the tree that is both man and woman, sun and moon. But to do so, we need to revive the sacredness of women, which is also the sacredness of the earth and the feminine powers of care, intuition, and healing within us all, regardless of gender. The voices of women who integrate the qualities of feminine wisdom into daily life are needed now more than ever. It's time to step out of the shadow—not with anger and retribution but with softness and courageous love.

It is my heartfelt priority to continue gathering the wisdom of women devoted to the Divine. This book and the Women Awakening Project are part of a growing movement to support and honor spirituality as told by women, in all its forms. The purpose is to spread sparks of grace across the world, to make the spiritual practice of nuns, saints, and laywomen more available, approachable, and accessible, and to inspire younger generations with virtuous female role models who remain connected with the mystery of nature and life as technology inevitably shapes a new path forward.

And as we break through the dome that has long enclosed us, we realize that whatever saves life is sacred—and that this sacred force is healing, joyful, and grace-bearing. This journey becomes a gentle invitation to all beings who feel in harmony with this approach—to live their lives as part of a fierce and tender, impersonal, and collective awakening. Like emissaries, each carrying her own light, we find ourselves flowing through arid lands, transforming generational paradigms, gently watering new fields and opening new pathways for a deeper integration between heaven and earth. In this unfolding, we come to realize that we are part of one vast and loving ocean of awareness.

Let us aspire to awaken this gentle, formidable power within us.

# ACKNOWLEDGMENTS

I am amazed at how much joy this book has brought into my life.

It has been a wonderful journey of discovery into the lives of human, divine, and exemplary women, into the being and fullness of life. I want to thank every person I have met on this path: From my beloved sisters in the yoga class in Rishikesh to the women I met along the way whom I interviewed but whose testimony did not fit into the space of this book. I want to thank the nuns of the Dongyu Gatsal Ling for their miraculous tsampa soup, which cured my sticky illness (it worked), and for the great inspiration offered by their dedication to their practice. I want to thank the sangha of the Amaravati Buddhist Monastery, the nuns of Thosamling, and the friends of the Ajatananda Ashram and the Santacittarama Buddhist monastery in Italy. Special thanks to my friend Rosa Dechen Lamo, with whom I shared truly unique moments in India, and Bethany May, who shared with me the longing for going forth as a nun. I also want to thank those who hosted me while I was writing this book. To Giovanni and Martina, who welcomed me into their beautiful house in the mountains of Pamparato, a place of peace and silence among the chestnut trees. And then there are Viviana and Andrea who always welcome me in Turin and believed in this project right from the start:

Thank you for being an inspiration by gathering the courage to take huge steps of freedom in your lives. Thanks also to Antonella Lumini for being a spiritual mother for me. And deep gratitude to Niharika Sanyal, who volunteered to polish my written Italian-English and edited this book with immense care. Immense gratitude to my editor Jenn Brown at Shambhala Publications for believing in this work and for striving to bring it to the best version of itself.

Thank you, Francesca, for your light that has been with me since I was born, and for supporting me in the first steps of creation of the Women Awakening Project. Thank you Chiara Sabattoli for offering insights and guidance on the development of the Women Awakening Project. Thanks to Margherita and Serena Aurora, who walk a bravely alternative path in life, and who remind me that living differently is not only possible but deeply meaningful.

Thank you, Daka, for all that we have gone through together. The flesh of this book comes directly from the blood we have shed. Thank you, Pål, for surprising me in love everyday. Thank you, Joshua and Peter, for showing up in Tuscany and supporting me magically on my way here. Thank you, Loic, for being by my side in the library of Tiruvannamalai and showing me what generosity means.

And thanks to all the women I interviewed, for they opened their hearts and shared the depth of their own experience with me. And thanks to all the donors who supported the Women Awakening Project with smaller and bigger donations for the realizations of the video tours in Italy, France, India, and the United States.

I could continue, and this list could be endless. Everything collaborated—everything encountered, everything given, lost, or received—I embrace you all in my heart. Thanks to my parents for always being there as earth and heaven and to my brother Mattia and his wife Anna.

Finally, thank you to those who have read these words. I hope that the voices in this book have taken you on a journey into the depths of yourselves and helped you regain faith in the greatness and wonder, in the spaciousness that we are.